For Quinn

To everyone in the Wood River and Sawtooth valleys who have
contributed their efforts, both physically and financially, to the
extensive trail systems we are able to enjoy.

Thank you.

A very special thanks to our family and friends for supporting us while writing Good Dirt II, and extra big
scruffs to Meg for always being up for another four-pawed adventure. We also can't forget the ever-
adventurous ride motivator, Chris, for his unimaginable desires to link-up every known and unknown trail
on the face of the earth.

We love you all!

Published by

Piñon Trading LLC
PO Box 600
Hailey, ID 83333

email: mcbob@sunvalley.net

web-site: www.idahoguidebooks.com

Library of Congress Cataloging-in-Publication Data
McRoberts, Greg
       Good Dirt II / by Greg McRoberts
         p.   cm.
       ISBN 0-9665953-2-7
       1. All terrain cycling - Idaho - Guidebooks. 2. All terrain cycling - Idaho - Sawtooth
National Recreation Area - Guidebooks. 3. Trails - Idaho - Guidebooks. 4. Idaho -
Guidebooks. I. Title. II. Title: Good Dirt II.

Other titles by Piñon Trading LLC include:
       Sun Spots - The Adventurous Travelers Guide to Sun Valley, Idaho
       A Weekend in Grandma's Underwear
       Have You Seen My Hair?

Cover design by Darla McRoberts
Book layout, design and authored by Greg McRoberts and Darla McRoberts
Original maps by E.B. Phillips / updated and new maps by Greg McRoberts

Need more information on what to do, where to stay, where to eat and where to hang when visiting the Sun Valley area? Purchase a copy of *Sun Spots*, at all local retailers throughout the Wood River and Sawtooth Valleys.

Table of Contents

Early mountain biking up Trail Creek outside Ketchum, circa 1945

Courtesy of Community Library, Ketchum, Idaho, Regional History Department

Good Dirt II Overview Map

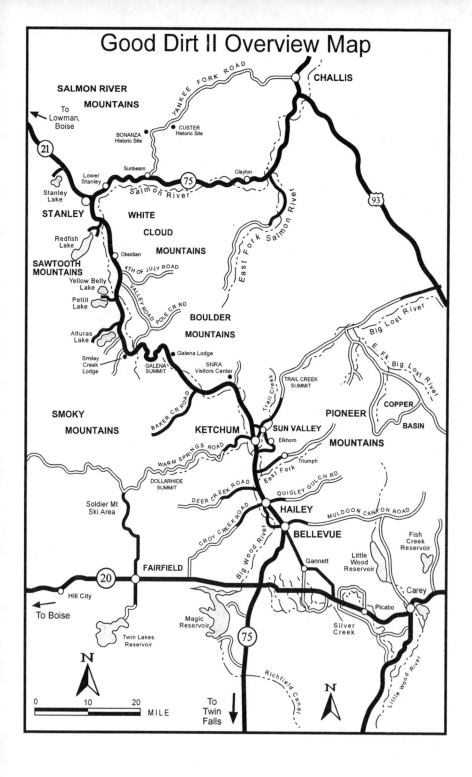

Ride Difficulty Level Cross Reference

Ride Difficulty Level Cross Reference

Moderate/Difficult Rides

Difficult Rides

Abusive & Gonzo Rides

About This Guidebook

Motorcyclists: Most people riding the trails around the Wood River and Sawtooth Valleys don't really know who have labored for years making and improving these incredible trails. It is the motorcycle riders who are unfortunately the ones who get crap for tearing up the trails and being loud in 'our' area. Well get over it Buckwheat. You wouldn't be on any of these trails if it weren't for their huge efforts in creating our trail systems and maintaining them on a yearly basis. So the next time you get passed by a group of motorcyclers having a great time, pull over, wave a nice hello and thank them for creating these awesome trails.

Ratings:

   Easy: A typical beginner, fun, cruiser ride for most any ability.
   Moderate: A bit harder than "easier" with most hills climbable, but not too technical.
   Difficult: Fairly technical ride with tough climbs and descents. You will feel worked afterwards.
   Abusive: The word speaks for itself, no matter the length of the ride. It is going to be hard, very technical, and you'll probably be in need of bandages.
   Gonzo: In an effort to define a new category, this one is beyond abusive. This means bring gear for a bivy, extra food, matches, water and clothing.

Ride Details:

   Length: We would hope this is self-explanatory. However, all rides have cyclometer (mileage) readings. We also list as many features as possible so the people riding without a cyclometer won't get lost.
   The Ride: Defines the ride as an out & back, loop or one-way.
   Surface: Explains the riding surface.
   Season: Tells you what time of year the ride is in it's best shape.
   Fun Factor: Key words to describe the highlights of the ride.
   Summary: Brief description of the ride to get you psyched up!

Tools/Clothing/Etc:

Hopefully, most of you are past getting dressed by your mothers each morning. Here is a small list of what to take just in case of some "interesting" weather.

   Clothing: Rain or wind jacket, tights, gloves, cap, helmet, durable footwear, and an extra fleece layer. Remember you are in the mountains here.
   Tools: Extra tubes, pump, patches, chain tool, tire levers, allen wrenches, spoke wrench, screw driver (both kinds) and a small crescent wrench.
   Misc. Items: More food and water than you think you need, first aid kit, emergency blanket and a camera (don't forget the film).
   HELMET: ALWAYS, ALWAYS, ALWAYS!!!!!!!!!!!!!!!

Information Accuracy (aka the standard disclaimer):

We try to be as accurate as possible. However, we are human, and can make mistakes in details, etc., no matter how many times we do a ride. Please let us know if there are any completely stupid mistakes in accuracy on anything in the guidebook. Keep in mind that the BLM, USFS and certain stealth individuals are continuously updating and creating new trails for your enjoyment. If you have any specific suggestions or corrections, please send them to: Piñon Trading LLC, PO Box 600, Hailey, ID 83333.

General Information

Ketchum Ranger District	208-622-5371
Stanley Ranger District	208-774-3681
Sawtooth National Recreation Area	208-726-7672
Lost River Ranger District	208-588-2224
Yankee Fork Ranger District	208-838-2201
Emergency	**911**

Camping

Camping in the Sun Valley and Stanley area is relatively easy. There are pay campgrounds and there are "primitive" non-pay campgrounds. Most dirt roads off Highway 75 lead to some sort of primitive camping, while all of the pay campgrounds are labeled with official USFS signs. Most fees range anywhere from $5-$7 per day. All campgrounds limit your stay to around 14 days maximum. The USFS rangers are happy to enforce your departure should you go beyond that time. If you're looking for a primitve campsite, take any dirt road north of Ketchum and you should be fine unless signs indicate otherwise. Please respect others and all private property. For more information on camping, hotels, etc. purchase a copy of *Sun Spots - The Adventurous Travelers Guide to Sun Valley, Idaho.*

Showers/Food/Hot Springs

So you stink and are hungry? No worries, we've got the places for you to chill out. Food, of course, is readily available in all the surrounding towns, as are motels, phones, etc. This is only as primitive as a place as you want it to be. Showers are available at a small cost in a couple areas: Redfish Lake, Easley Hot Springs, Sun Valley Athletic Club. Hot springs are dotted along the Salmon River north, west and east of Stanley, as well as up Warm Springs Road west of Ketchum. A special note on the hot springs: don't pee, poo, litter or detour the flow of or in any of the hot springs. Mother Nature put them here for us to enjoy, so please don't spoil it for the rest of the world.

Bugs & Animals

All of the rides in this guidebook are in the mountains where mosquitos, bees and other flying (stinging) insects live. Most repellents work great at knocking them off their wings. Be careful in the later part of summer for hornets and bees who tend to migrate toward open carbonated sugar drinks and beer. We also have a large population of big game animals. The elk, moose, deer, bear, wolf, fox, coyotes and all the other furry little creatures were here first. Remember that we are the ones playing in their homes and space. Please respect them and their privacy. Anyone caught harassing the animals will be stripped, tarred and feathered and paraded up and down main street in Ketchum on the hood of Johnny Law's car.

Other Activities

Welcome to resort town life where there are always activites happening to keep you busy when you're off the saddle or when it rains. There are four movie theatres between Ketchum and Hailey, bars everywhere, plenty of restaurants, horseback riding, world famous whitewater kayaking, paragliding, rafting and trails that offer great hiking to high alpine lakes. Don't forget your fishing gear. Fly-fishing is one of this areas main attractions. How about a round of golf on one of our world class golf courses? Remember this is a destination resort designed to keep you and your money happy. For specific information, purchase a copy of the local guidebook *Sun Spots-The Adventurous Travelers Guide to Sun Valley, Idaho.*

A Bit About Central Idaho History

This part of central Idaho has a very rich history in mining. Around the lower part of the Wood River valley (Ketchum, Hailey, Bellevue), you can see mining scars, tailings and trails on the sides of some incredibly steep terrain. This is our mining past. Several rides in this guidebook lead to mining ghost towns such as Sawtooth City, Vienna, Custer, etc. In fact, back in the 1800's some of the populations of these mining communities were bigger than Ketchum is today.

In the Stanley area, prospectors and hermits were a big part of the scene. They made their living by trying to strike it rich with their mining claims or just living in the wilderness year-round on the Middle Fork of the Salmon River. These hearty people led a rugged lifestyle, usually seeing other humans only once or twice a year.

Idaho is known as "The Wilderness State," with over 16 million acres of wildland. This is more than any other state aside from Alaska. The Sawtooth Mountains, in the heart of the Sawtooth National Wilderness Area, are a huge attraction in the summertime benefiting backpackers, rock and alpine climbers as well as casual day hikers. However, these beautiful spires are not just for summer pleasure. They also offer great backcountry skiing in the winter and early springtime. But do take note: no mountain bikes or motorized vehicles are allowed in the Sawtooth Wilderness Area. So please respect the boundary signs and laws or Ranger Rick will be happy to do it for you. For more information on our local/state history, visit one of the bookstores in town. They all have a great selection of books.

Weather and Lightning

The mountains in the springtime can offer some of the most incredibly gorgeous scenery with wildflowers blooming and mountain streams flowing at full force. But don't be fooled by Mother Nature. June, July and August in central Idaho have a history of afternoon thunder storms that gather rapidly on the western horizon. Those small dark clouds in the distance can be upon you in no time, dumping rain, hail and even snow. So be prepared for anything. Always bring a rain jacket, extra food and water.

Another springtime worry in the mountains is lightning. "Oh, what are the chances," you ask? Actually, the chance of getting struck by lightning is very remote, but possible. Take all the necessary precautions when you begin to hear thunder and see lightning. Lightning is usually at the leading edge of a storm where it is most violent. If you are not sure that electricity is in the air, check some obvious signs.

Take your helmet off and if your hair is standing on end, then yes, there is electricity in the area. You can also check the hair on your arms and smell ozone in the air. Obvious question here, what does ozone smell like? Much different than the clear mountain air you've been breathing, almost like a wet dog (we're not kidding). If you get caught in an electric storm, do the following: make yourself small to minimize contact points with the ground (squat), get off any ridges, get away from lone trees, lake shores, and rock outcroppings. If someone is struck by lightning, (hopefully you know first aid) rush to get help. Due to the fact that we could get sued for telling you how to treat an injury, we can't say anything here. **Remember:** DON'T GO OUT UNPREPARED FOR ANY EMERGENCY. You may be close to a town, but you are still miles away in a wild area and help can be just that much further away... "Be smart," as my dad would say.

Mountain Biking Ethics

The Authors Version: Do unto others as you would want them to do unto you and your bike. In other words, don't be a jerk on the trails. Yield to everyone, uphill traffic, horses, hikers and other cyclists. Treat our trails the way you eat in your mothers living room. Help out others in need of tools, water, etc. This isn't the World Cup or Olympics, this is a peaceful place, so chill out, put your adrenaline aside and relax.

The IMBA Version: Ride on open trails only. Leave no trace. Control your bicycle. Always yield the trail. Never spook Animals. Plan ahead.

DO NOT SKID, this deteriorates and erodes the trails making them useless. Push up or lower your bike down instead. Skidding around switchbacks is not the proper technique. Push your limits and when you reach the high end, push your bike.

DESCEND UNDER CONTROL to avoid skidding, trail erosion, hitting an other trail user and an expensive trip to the emergency room (remember 911).

STAY OFF WET TRAILS. This does not pertain to just "closed" trails in early season, since riding after a rain storm or snow melt can completely ruin a trail.

YIELD TO EVERYONE. Like it states above, this is a peaceful place we live in, so please be courteous to everyone or thing you encounter on the trails. Horses have very poor eyesight and are easily spooked. We have very poor eyesight and are easily spooked. Please be careful.

Trail Updates

You can log onto our web-site anytime and get current trail conditions, when trails are open, closed, etc. This site also lists any new trails and suggestions for the serious adventure riders:

http://www.idahoguidebooks.com

WRASTA

Wood River Area Single Track Association

This organization was formed in 1999 to help with the establishment and maintenance of the trail systems throughout the Wood River Valley. Through years of use and abuse, our trails need constant maintenance and upkeep. Unfortunately this is not free or cheap. Funds are constantly required to pay for tools, materials and labor with the USFS, private individuals and private businesses hired to do trail work. Without money, existing trails are not maintained and new trails do not get developed. This is where we need your help.

By joining WRASTA, you can help us keep our trails in the shape they need to be in for everyone to enjoy year after year. Individual membership is only $10 and is renewable every two years. Business membership is $25, and family membership is $20. This is not a scam or a waste of your money. The money goes directly to the USFS and private businesses to develop and maintain our trail systems. In fact, 10% of the proceeds from the sale of this book go directly to that same fund. So dig deep and put out. *Join WRASTA today.*

membership information

Name of individual/family/business:_____

Address:_____

City:_____ST:_____Zip:_____

Email:_____

☐ I am joining as an individual $10/two years.

☐ We are joining as a family $20/two years.

☐ We are joining as a business $25/two years.

☐ Yes, I want a membership card sent to me!

☐ Yes, I want to be notified for the next fund-raising event.

☐ Yes, I want my name listed in the next edition of Good Dirt as a member/contributor.

☐ Yes, I want to donate more than my membership. $50 ☐ $100 ☐ $250 ☐

Please send this form to:

Pinon Trading LLC
PO Box 600
Hailey, ID 83333

SUN VALLEY

- Eclectic Menu -

Asian   Aged Steaks

Mexican   Burgers

Italian   Salads

Pizza   Wraps

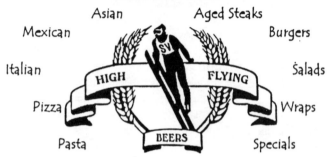

Pasta   Specials

Appetizers   Homemade Desserts

- Hand~Crafted Ales & Lagers -

BREWING COMPANY

202 North Main Street ~ Hailey

788~0805

Looking north on Hailey Main Street, circa 1920
Courtesy of Wood River Journal

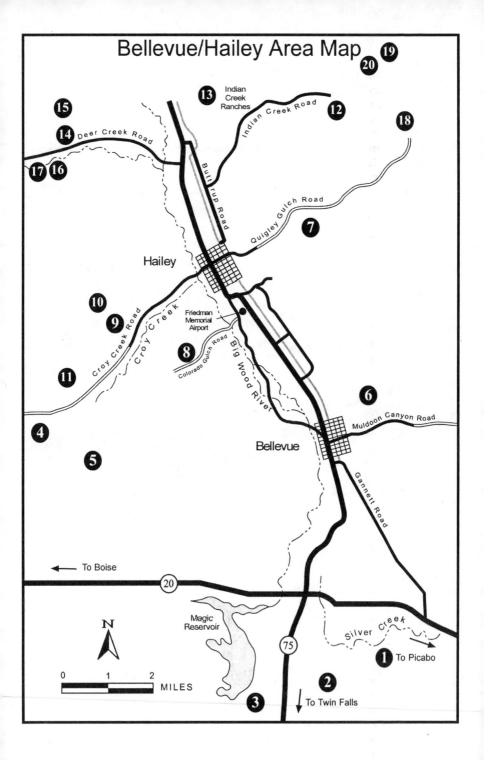

Bellevue/Hailey Area Map

18

1. Silver Creek

Length: 33.2 miles
Starting Elevation: 5000'
High Point Elevation: 5150'
Total Elevation Gain: 325'
The Ride: Loop
Surface: Dirt jeep road and pavement
Difficulty Rating: Easy
Season: Late March - late November
Fun Factor: Cruiser, sagebrush, desert wildlife & flowers.
Summary: For a great early or late season ride, this is the one. Fast dirt roads and cruising corners make this loop attractive to those who have cabin fever!
Getting There: From Hailey, drive south on Hwy 75 to Bellevue. At the southern end of town, turn left onto Gannett Road, which is just across from Sawtooth Wood Products. Drive past the town of Gannett (about 6+ miles) to the junction with Hwy 20. Turn left here and go another 4 miles to Picabo. Park on the left at the Silver Creek Store (be sure to park in the back of the parking area to avoid taking up their valuable space). The ride begins here.

<u>Miles</u>	<u>The Ride</u>:
0.0	Cross over Hwy 20, and ride on the west side of the grain silos, turning left just after them and over the canal. Go another 2 blks and turn right on Robert St.
1.0	Pass a couple of ranches on the right.
1.8	Cross over the cattle guard and begin the desert riding.
3.1	Take the left fork where the spur road takes off straight ahead.
4.0	Cross another cattle guard and continue through the fence.
7.5	Cross yet another cattle guard and fence (great desert views straight ahead). Yes, that is the grassy road straight in front of you.
8.3	After crossing another cattle guard, stay straight. The right fork goes nowhere.
9.3	Big fork! Stay right, and head up a small incline. Shortly thereafter, go left at the small fork, paralleling the fence.
11.1	Cross another cattle guard and fence.
11.9	At the fork, stay left. The right fork goes to a view pt and the radio towers on top of the mtn overlooking the entire area.
13.6	Another fork. Go right and up to the small saddle.
14.2	A saddle with a view.
15.9	Wow, another cattle guard and fence crossing.
17.2	Yet another cattle guard and fence crossing then up a small hill. The Lunar Ridge Flight Park for paragliding and hang-gliding is located on the ridge to the right.
18.5	Cattle guard and fence.
19.9	Junction with Hwy 75. Go right and down Timmerman Hill towards Bellevue (be careful of all traffic).
21.2	At the flashing light at the bottom of the hill, turn right onto Hwy 20 towards Picabo and Carey.
29.2	After passing the second Gannett Road (yes, there were two of them), go another 4 more miles to the Silver Creek Store.
33.2	The end of the ride.

Silver Creek

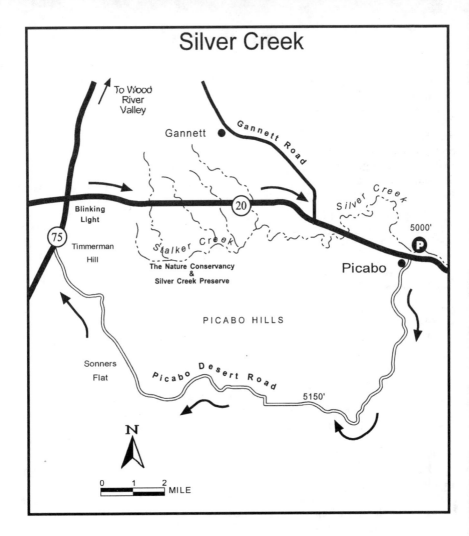

To Wood River Valley

Gannett   Gannett Road

Blinking Light

Timmerman Hill

Stalker Creek

The Nature Conservancy
&
Silver Creek Preserve

Silver Creek

5000'
P

Picabo

PICABO HILLS

Sonners Flat

Picabo Desert Road

5150'

N

0   1   2 MILE

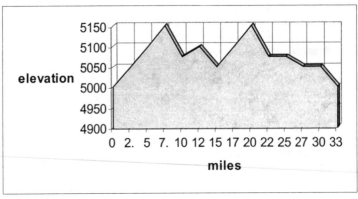

elevation

5150
5100
5050
5000
4950
4900

0 2. 5 7. 10 12 15 17 20 22 25 27 30 33

miles

2. Sonners Flat

Length: 12.3 miles
Starting Elevation: 4950'
High Point Elevation: 5050'
Total Elevation Gain: 100'
The Ride: Loop
Surface: Dirt jeep road
Difficulty Rating: Easy
Season: Late March - late November
Fun Factor: Spring wildflowers, desert life and potential wildlife.
Summary: This is a kick-in-the-butt quick early or late season cruise of a ride. Early season gives the potential for wildlife around the watering hole near the end of the ride.
Getting There: From Hailey, drive south on Hwy 75 approximately 21 miles to Picabo Desert Road. Turn left here and park immediately on the right, the ride begins here.

Miles	The Ride:
0.0	Begin by heading east on the Picabo Desert Road.
0.7	At the first fork, go left toward the rock outcroppings.
0.9	At the fork, stay straight (right) and NOT left like the sign indicates, you'll meet up with it in a moment.
1.2	Take the left fork like the sign says, heading in a northerly direction. From here, the road becomes a bit faint, and a bit rocky following the natural gas pipeline. No smoking or farting please.
2.9	Big spur road on the right. Stay straight following the pipeline.
4.9	At the junction with a major dirt road, turn right here and begin cruising in an easterly direction. The Lunar Ridge Flight Park for paragliding and hang-gliding is located on the ridge to the left.
7.0	Major intersection. Stay to the right turning westward.
11.6	At the fork, stay left rejoining your original loop.
12.3	The end of the ride and back at your car.

Sonners Flat

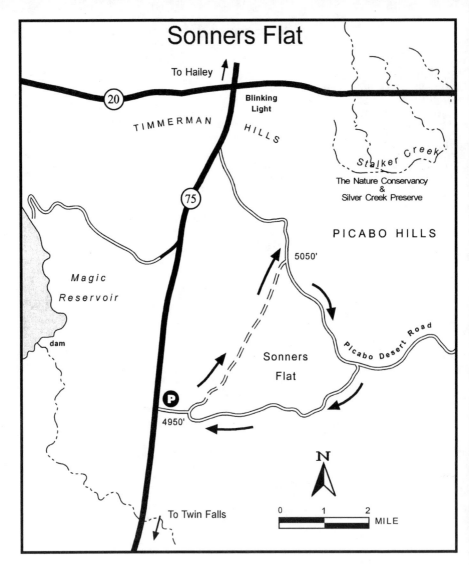

To Hailey

20

TIMMERMAN

Blinking
Light

HILLS

75

Stalker Creek

The Nature Conservancy
&
Silver Creek Preserve

PICABO HILLS

5050'

Magic
Reservoir

dam

Picabo Desert Road

Sonners
Flat

P

4950'

N

To Twin Falls

0   1   2
MILE

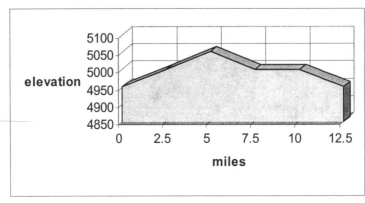

elevation

5100
5050
5000
4950
4900
4850

0   2.5   5   7.5   10   12.5

miles

3. Dinosaur Ridge

Length: 6.4 miles
Starting Elevation: 4800'
High Point Elevation: 4950'
Total Elevation Gain: 150'
The Ride: Loop
Surface: Dirt jeep road
Difficulty Rating: Easy
Season: Late March - late November
Fun Factor: Big Wood River, wildlife, wildflowers, lava rocks.
Summary: Another great desert ride.
Getting There: From Hailey, drive south on Hwy 75 for approximately 23 miles and turn right at the BLM sign for the "Upper Big Wood River Access." Follow this road to the first fork and go left. At the second fork, a short bit later, turn right into the parking area next to the river and bathroom. The ride begins here.

Miles	The Ride:
0.0	Begin by riding north across the parking area and onto a faint jeep trail which immediately crosses a fence. Please close the gate.
0.2	At the first fork, stay to the right.
0.5	At the second fork, stay to the right . . . again.
1.0	Turn left onto the single-track trail and go up onto the old railroad grade where you turn left again paralleling where you just came from. After a short distance cross through another fence.
2.4	Turn right just before this seemingly endless straight road comes to an end and plunges off the cliff into the river. Cross the main dirt road and head in a northerly direction toward a lava rock saddle.
3.4	After gaining the small saddle, take the right fork and turn right (again) at the small rock cairn onto a much less traveled road. Trust me.
3.8	Yes, it's a fence. Do a bunny-hop over it (just kidding). Lift your bike over the fence and continue down the other side, staying on the west side of Dinosaur Ridge on the obvious jeep road.
4.8	At the junction with the main dirt road, turn left and continue across a cow-guard.
5.2	At the big fork, take a right heading back toward your car.
6.1	Take a right again at the fork toward the river and your car.
6.4	Cross the cow-guard, grab the checkered flag and that's the end of the ride.

Dinosaur Ridge

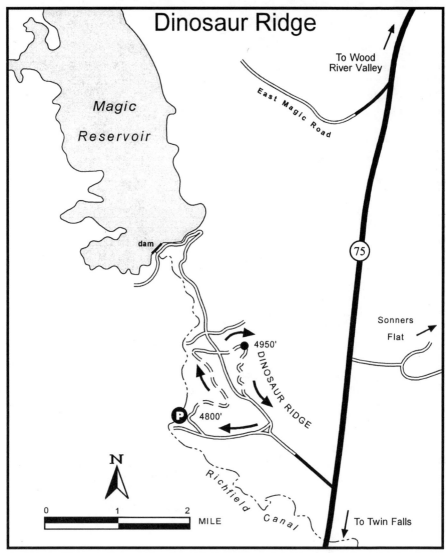

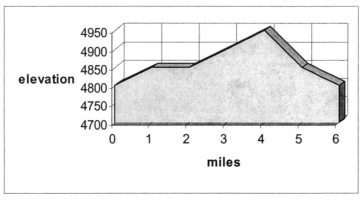

4. Hatty Gulch

Length: 26.2 miles
Starting Elevation: 5300'
High Point Elevation: 6000'
Total Elevation Gain: 1110'
The Ride: Loop
Surface: Dirt jeep road, pavement, single track
Difficulty Rating: Easy/Moderate
Season: Late April - late November
Fun Factor: The serene sagebrush desert setting with cow pies and water.
Summary: This is the standard locals early season ride to get their legs and butt into shape. It's a fast cruise with minimal climbing, all on jeep road.
Getting There: From Hailey Main Street, turn left (west) onto Bullion St at the street light and go 1.5 blocks to Hop Porter Park. This is where the ride begins. A shorter ride option is to drive to the junction with Rock Creek Road and begin the ride there.

Miles	**The Ride:**
0.0	Begin by riding out Croy Creek on the pavement, passing through housing areas and the BMX track. Watch for Rotorun Ski Area on the right.
3.7	The pavement ends and the dirt road begins. Stay straight on this road.
4.1	Pass by Rock Creek Road on the left. Stay straight, this is where you complete the loop.
9.1	Just before starting to climb up Richardson Summit, turn left and follow this road down, passing by a "danger, open mines" sign.
9.3	Turn right on the switchback and follow the road down into the main gulch following the stream bed. You will follow this main Hatty gulch all the way to the junction with Rock Creek Road. There may be new fencing, bad ruts and cows in your way, but stick to the road which follows the stream flow and you'll be fine.
18.5	The junction with Rock Creek Road. Turn left and begin some gradual climbing up toward Rocky Butte. Stay on this main road all the way up and over.
22.1	The junction with Croy Creek Road and your loop is complete. Follow Croy all the way back to Hailey.
26.2	Back at Hop Porter Park in Hailey and a job well done.

Hatty Gulch

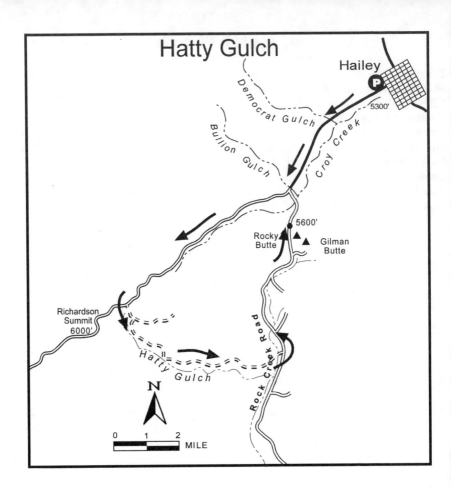

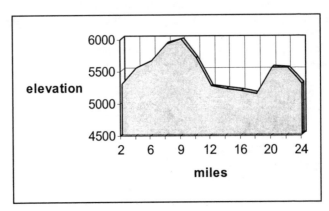

5. Rock Creek to Poverty Flats

Length: 32.8 miles
Starting Elevation: 5300'
High Point Elevation: 5600'
Total Elevation Gain: 700'
The Ride: Loop
Surface: Dirt jeep road and pavement
Difficulty Rating: Easy/Moderate (due to length)
Season: Early April - late November
Fun Factor: Fast cruiser through sage, wildflowers and small canyons.
Summary: This is the best early season ride around taking you through some remote drainages all the while staying close to the Wood River Valley.
Getting There: From Hailey, park anywhere around Main Street (Highway 75) and Bullion near the stop light. Don't abuse the 2 hour parking limit in certain areas. An alternative is to park 1 block behind Pauls Grocery Store at Hop Porter Park.

<u>Miles</u>	<u>The Ride</u>:
0.0	From the stop light in Hailey, head west on Bullion Street and pass over the Big Wood River.
1.2	You are now in Croy Creek Canyon passing by the Wood River Animal Shelter. Stay on this main road for 3.5 miles.
4.7	Turn left at the junction with Rock Creek Road and head in a southwesterly direction.
5.4	Stay left at the fork.
6.1	You gain the saddle next to Rocky Butte overlooking Rock Creek. Over the next 3+ miles stay on the main road paralleling Rock Creek at all times. Sky Ridge Flight Park for paragliding and hang-gliding is on the ridge to the left
9.8	Cross over the creek and continue riding next to an old paddock (pasture).
12.7	Pass by an old red barn on the right.
14.9	After the cattle guard, the road forks, go left in an easterly direction.
17.2	Begin a steady climb upward to a saddle.
18.0	Gain the saddle and enjoy a great view of the southern part of the Wood River Valley.
20.0	Pass by some houses and begin your reintroduction to society. From here always stay on the main road as it winds through a country-living area.
23.2	Intersection with the pavement of Glendale Road. Go left here.
24.4	Pass by a gravel pit on the right and immediately over the Big Wood River.
24.9	Intersection with Highway 75. Turn left here and stay on the shoulder of the highway on into Bellevue. Be careful!
27.2	Welcome to Bellevue. Turn right on Chestnut St. and turn left immediately onto the bike path. Start pedaling north through Bellevue and eventually to Hailey.
32.5	Turn left off the bike path onto Bullion Street and back to Hailey downtown.
32.8	End of ride and back in Hailey.

Rock Creek to Poverty Flats

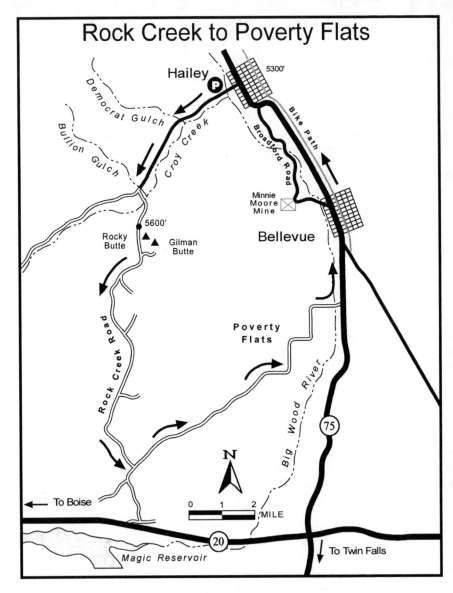

Hailey

5300'

Democrat Gulch

Bullion Gulch

Croy Creek

Broadford Road

Bike Path

Minnie Moore Mine

Bellevue

5600'

Rocky Butte

Gilman Butte

Rock Creek Road

Poverty Flats

Big Wood River

75

N

To Boise

0   1   2   MILE

20

To Twin Falls

Magic Reservoir

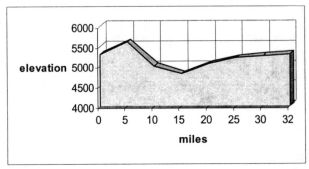

elevation

6000
5500
5000
4500
4000

0   5   10   15   20   25   30   32

miles

6. Slaughterhouse Creek

Length: 13 miles
Starting Elevation: 5230'
High Point Elevation: 6200'
Total Elevation Gain: 970'
The Ride: Out & back
Surface: Dirt jeep road
Difficulty Rating: Easy
Season: April - November
Fun Factor: Beautiful canyon with alpine meadows.
Summary: This is a casual ride through an unspoiled Southern canyon with alpine meadows, groves of aspens and five quick stream crossings (just to add a bit of excitement).
Getting There: From Hailey, drive south on Hwy 75 to Bellevue and turn east on Cedar Street, which is the street next to the old white building with a steeple that looks like an old church but is really the old Bellevue City Hall. Stay straight on this road, crossing the bike path and the elementary school on the left. Drive to the top of the hill and park anywhere out of the way of the road and driveways. The ride begins here.

<u>Miles</u>	<u>The Ride:</u>
0.0	Begin by riding up the north side of the canyon.
0.2	Spur road on the right, stay straight.
1.4	Steep spur road takes off on the left which eventually hooks up with the spur road that takes off on the left at mile 1.5. Stay on the main road here.
2.7	A few springs muddy up the road a bit here (not bad). After some big shade trees, motor up a steep climb. From here the road crosses the creek five times over the next 2 miles.
4.8	You're at the last of the stream crossings.
5.0	Spur road up the canyon on the right, stay on the main road.
5.7	After the canyon narrows, it opens again fairly soon.
6.5	Fork in the road and the top of the ride for those of you joining us for the Out & Back portion of the movie. Those of you who want to call it good, turn around and ride the 6.5 miles back to the trailhead . . . thanks for playing. The left fork continues up the drainage (very rutted) to the saddle with Quigley Creek and down into Hailey. See the ride: Quigley Creek to Slaughterhouse Creek for more information.
13.0	Back at your car in Bellevue.

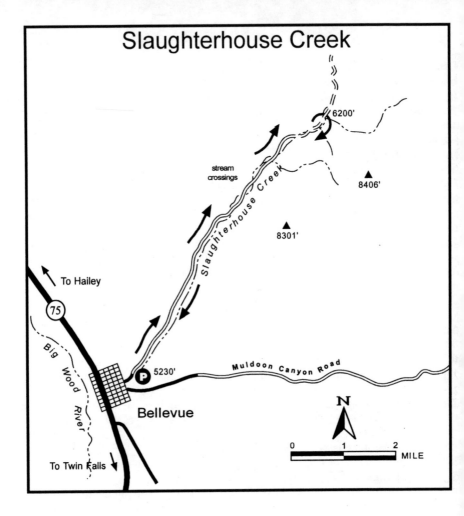

Slaughterhouse Creek

To Hailey

75

Big Wood River

To Twin Falls

Bellevue

stream crossings

Slaughterhouse Creek

6200'

8406'

8301'

5230'

Muldoon Canyon Road

N

0   1   2   MILE

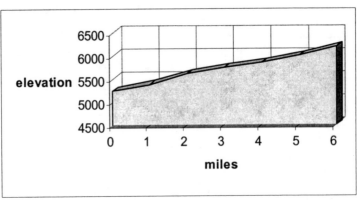

elevation

6500
6000
5500
5000
4500

0   1   2   3   4   5   6

miles

7. Quigley Creek to Slaughterhouse Creek

Length: 19.2 miles
Starting Elevation: 5350'
High Point Elevation: 6950'
Total Elevation Gain: 1600'
The Ride: Loop
Surface: Dirt jeep road
Difficulty Rating: Moderate/Difficult
Season: April - November
Fun Factor: Easy rolling ride through a serene canyon setting with good climbing.
Summary: This is a great non-technical ride with moderate elevation gain near the top end. If this were aerobics, it would be classified as "low impact."
Getting There: From the stop light at Bullion St and Hwy 75 in downtown Hailey, drive 1 block South to Croy Street and turn left here. After half a mile, follow the road around a natural right turn and take an immediate left onto Quigley Road, which is directly in front of the "Deerfield" sign. Continue forward to where the pavement turns to dirt and park here.

Miles	The Ride:
0.0	Begin riding up Quigley Creek Road heading east along side a large field and across the cattle guard.
1.75	Pass the Quigley Pond on the right side of the road.
2.2	Small spur road on the right, continue straight on Quigley Creek Road.
2.5	The spur road rejoins the main road.
4.2	Pass a corral then a spur road just a bit further on the left side.
5.8	Spur road on the left leads to/from Indian Creek. Continue up the main road curving to the south up and through some clear cuts. Always stay on the main road through this area. For more information see the *Indian Creek to Quigley Creek* ride.
7.6	Small private cabin appears off to the right.
7.8	At the fork in the road before a small creek (possibly dry in mid to late summer), turn right on the spur road, traversing back across the hillside. If you were to turn left or stay on the main road here, you would be on the *Quigley Creek to Cove Creek* ride.
8.3	You've reached the saddle overlooking Slaughterhouse Creek. Continue down the other rutted side of the saddle and toward Bellevue.
9.5	After crossing the small creek, stay to the right heading down the canyon toward Bellevue. For the next 6.5 miles you'll have many stream crossings and a few mud-bogs, otherwise it's a straight shot down the canyon into Bellevue. Be careful since there can be heavily eroded obstacles on this part of the downhill.
16.0	The end of the dirt road and the town of Bellevue. Continue down Cedar Street until you get to the Wood River Bike Trail. Turn right. Ride approximately 3.2 miles into Hailey and turn right on Croy Street and retrace your steps to your car at the mouth of Quigley Creek.
19.2	End of the loop (hopefully in one piece) and back at your car.

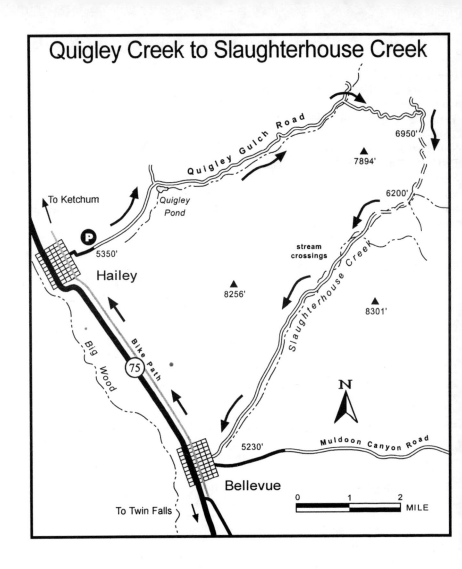

Quigley Creek to Slaughterhouse Creek

To Ketchum

Quigley Gulch Road

Quigley Pond

6950'

7894'

6200'

P

5350'

stream crossings

Slaughterhouse Creek

Hailey

8256'

8301'

Big Wood

Bike Path

75

N

5230'

Muldoon Canyon Road

Bellevue

To Twin Falls

0   1   2   MILE

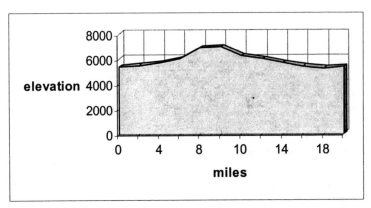

elevation

8000
6000
4000
2000
0

0   4   8   10   14   18

miles

8. Colorado Gulch

Length: 8.2 miles
Starting Elevation: 5300'
High Point Elevation: 6250'
Total Elevation Gain: 950'
The Ride: Loop
Surface: Dirt jeep road and pavement
Difficulty Rating: Moderate/Difficult
Season: Mid-April - November
Fun Factor: A quick pump, a quick downhill and you're back on the couch.
Summary: If you have a need for a very quick workout to kill some of that daily stress, jump on this ride and don't get off.
Getting There: From the stop light at Bullion St and Hwy 75 in downtown Hailey, drive one block west (behind Pauls Grocery) to Hop Porter Park. The ride begins here.

Miles	**The Ride:**
0.0	Begin by riding back up to Main Street in Hailey (Hwy 75) and head south toward the airport. Turn right on Cedar St, just before the Post Office, then a quick left onto Broadford Rd. Go 0.8 miles and turn right on a dirt road (don't take the right just before the old abandoned wood house. Insead take the second, more beaten dirt road after the old wood house). Go down the road veering left and crossing the bridge over the Big Wood River and begin climbing through aspens next to the creek.
2.8	After passing several spur roads on either side of the road, pass a mine and old buildings on the left.
3.8	With some steady climbs behind you, the trail levels out for a spell before climbing again.
4.1	Top of the ride. Congrats, catch your breath and get ready for a speedy ride downhill.
5.5	Junction with Croy Creek Road. Turn right (east) back toward Hailey, stay ing on Croy Creek Road all the way back to Main Street stop light in Hailey.
8.2	Just after crossing the Big Wood River, you'll see Hop Porter Park on the left and your car. This is the end of the ride.

SIERRA DESIGNS
www.SIERRADESIGNS.com

Colorado Gulch

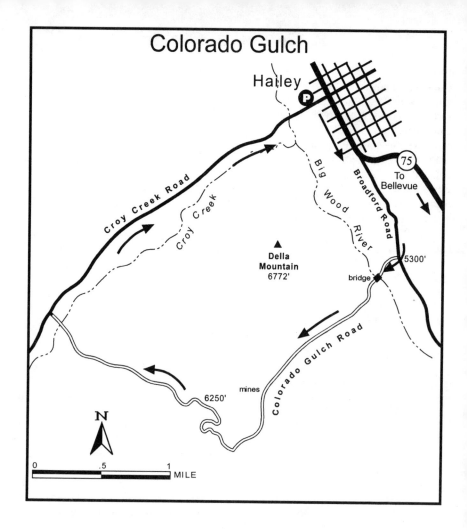

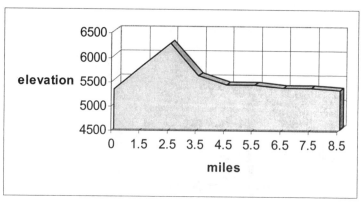

34

9. Democrat Gulch

Length: 12.4 miles
Starting Elevation: 5300'
High Point Elevation: 6750'
Total Elevation Gain: 750' or 1450' (750' to the first turn around)
The Ride: Out and back
Surface: Pavement to dirt jeep road
Difficulty Rating: Moderate/Difficult to top, or 'Easy' to first turn around.
Season: Early April - late October
Fun Factor: Small but beautiful creek, Pioneer Mountain views, wildflowers.
Summary: So, you need a change of pace from that boring single-track riding? This is it. Casual or difficult, you make the choice, and either one well worth it.
Getting There: From the stop light at Bullion St and Hwy 75 in downtown Hailey, park 1 block behind Pauls Grocery Store at Hop Porter Park. The ride begins here.

Miles	The Ride:
0.0	From the stop light in Hailey, head west on Bullion Street, quickly crossing over the Big Wood River.
1.2	You are now in Croy Creek Canyon passing by the Wood River Animal Shelter.
1.7	Turn right onto Democrat Gulch road and wind up the side of a small hill. There may or may not be other cars parked at this make-shift trailhead.
2.0	A gravel road enters in from the left. Stay on main road.
2.9	Spur road on the right goes up Two-Dog Loop. Notice a small pond on the left. Remember, stay on the main road.
3.9	Spur road on the right, don't take it.
4.1	Beaver ponds on the left.
4.7	Enter into the rocky corridor, you'll know what we mean.
5.0	Cross over the creek on an exposed pipe... careful.
5.2	Fork in the road after crossing over the creek. The left road goes nowhere. Take the right fork and begin a gradual climb to the top. This can also be a turn-around point for the more casual version of this ride, otherwise continue on up. (6050')
6.2	This is the top of the ride. You can check out the Pioneer Mountains to the East, or explore the other trails up here. Be careful descending back down the gulch and into Hailey.
12.4	Back in Hailey and the end of the ride.

Democrat Gulch

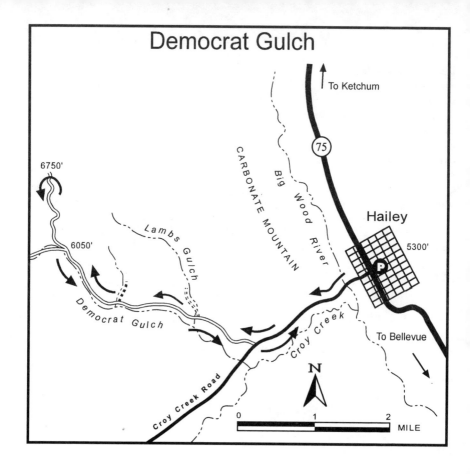

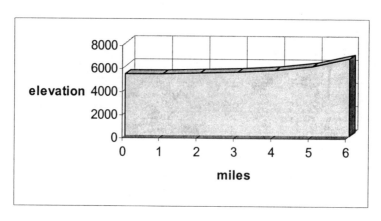

10. Two-Dog Loop

Length: 8.3 miles
Starting Elevation: 5300'
High Point Elevation: 6220'
Total Elevation Gain: 1050'
The Ride: Loop
Surface: Dirt jeep road, single-track, pavement
Difficulty Rating: Moderate
Fun Factor: Good for early season and late fall in a peaceful setting.
Summary: Close to Hailey single-track that'll get your heart pounding, your legs burning and a smile on your face afterwards. This ride is named for the memory of Candi and Broadie, and besides, most people have at least two dogs with them here!
Getting There: From the stop light at Bullion St and Hwy 75 in downtown Hailey, drive west into the large canyon aptly named Croy Canyon. At 1.7 miles, park on the right side of the road next to the dirt road and fence. Please don't block the road.

Miles	The Ride:
0.0	Begin by riding up the dirt road (quick hill) that you parked next to. Stay on this road for the next 1 mile.
1.0	Turn right just past the trees onto a jeep road which crosses the stream.
2.0	After crossing a cattle guard and another stream, stay left at the next junction.
2.5	In the small clearing cross the creek, stay left and begin a short climb up.
2.8	The top of the climb. Descend the opposite side of the saddle on a faint jeep trail which turns to single-track shortly. On the grassy hill, make your way down the semi-non-existent trail to the grove of trees. There, you will find a better single-track trail leading down the canyon on the <u>east</u> side of the creek.
3.7	Junction with Democrat Gulch Road. Turn right here.
3.8	Whoa! Look for the single-track dropping down to the left and crossing the creek, which is located where the willows are closest to the road.
4.2	The top of the first saddle. The trail forks shortly afterwards. Both trails lead to the same place a hundred yards later, but be careful of loose rocks.
4.8	Cross over the dry stream bed and follow the faint trail leading left and up.
5.0	Top of the second saddle. Careful for the sharp turn on the descent.
5.5	In the clearing with houses down to the left, stay straight and continue traversing up on the double track jeep road.
5.7	Top of the last saddle overlooking the BMX track area. There become many trails all over the place as you descend. Stay on the most popular path, watch for glass and head for the left (east) of the BMX track area, and watch out for broken glass.
6.4	Junction with Croy Creek Road. Turn left and follow this road back to your car at the start of Democrat Gulch.
8.3	Yep, you're here, the end of the ride. Nice job!

(This ride is sponsored by WRASTA - Wood River Area Single Track Association)

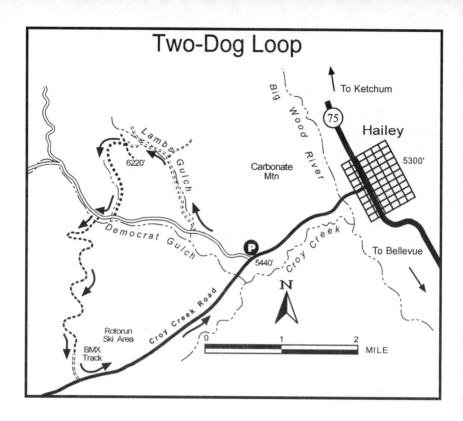

Two-Dog Loop

To Ketchum

Hailey

5300'

Big Wood River

Carbonate Mtn

75

Lambs Gulch

6220'

Democrat Gulch

P

5440'

Croy Creek

Croy Creek Road

To Bellevue

Rotorun Ski Area

BMX Track

N

0   1   2   MILE

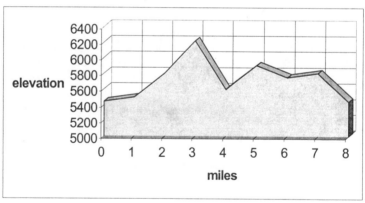

elevation

6400
6200
6000
5800
5600
5400
5200
5000

0 1 2 3 4 5 6 7 8

miles

11. Bullion Gulch

Length: 6.8 miles
Starting Elevation: 5550'
High Point Elevation: 6400'
Total Elevation Gain: 850'
The Ride: Out and back
Surface: Dirt jeep road
Difficulty Rating: Moderate
Season: Mid April - late October
Fun Factor: Old mines, wildlife and wildflowers by the creek.
Summary: Bullion Gulch is such a casual, fun ride, I'm surprised it's not more popular. With slow rollers up the canyon, you'll have a great experience (ultimately reaching the mines).
Getting There: From Hailey, drive west out Bullion Street and into Croy Creek Canyon. After 4.6 miles, park on the right and out of the way at the beginning of Bullion Gulch road (**Mining road construction could be in progress, please be careful).

<u>Miles</u>	<u>The Ride</u>:
0.0	Begin by riding up Bullion Gulch Road at a slight grade.
0.8	Ride through the new Bullion Gulch subdivision.
2.5	Huge mining tailings on the left.
2.8	As the road forks, take the right fork since the left one vanishes quickly.
3.4	Ah yes, welcome to the Bullion Gulch mining ruins. This is the top of the ride. The road continues up for just over one-half mile further, then peters out at a spring. If you are into exploring the mines, please be careful and don't enter into any shafts or buildings as they are either collapsed or in the process thereof.Turn around here and head on back down the road.
6.8	End of the ride and at your car at the bottom of Bullion Gulch.

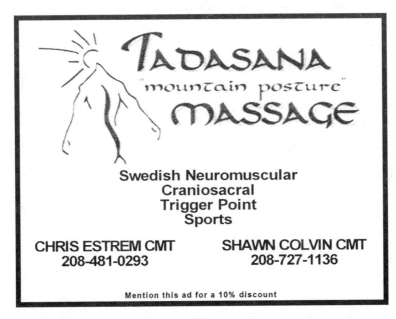

Bullion Gulch

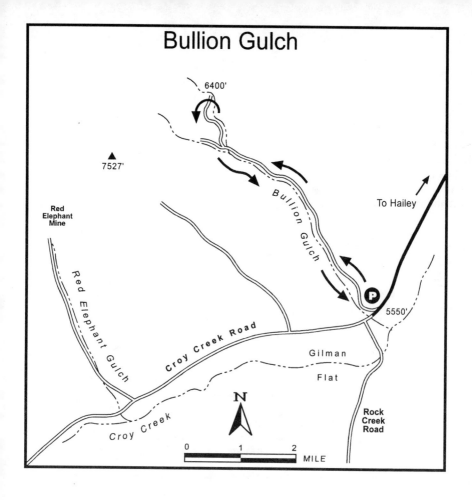

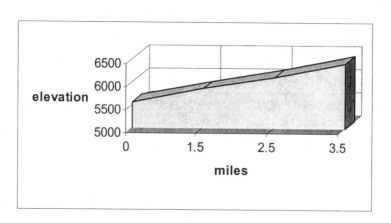

12. Indian Creek to Quigley Creek

Length: 18.6
Starting Elevation: 5397'
High Point Elevation: 7310'
Total Elevation Gain: 1913'
The Ride: Loop
Surface: Pavement and dirt jeep road
Difficulty Rating: Moderate/Difficult
Season: Late April - October
Fun Factor: Fun hill-climbs, killer views and an awesome descent!
Summary: This can be as intense as you make it. Stop often on the climb and enjoy yourself, or abuse yourself and do it non-stop. Once the climb is over, this is an amazing downhill all the way back to Hailey. (**Some people like to do this ride opposite of how it's written here.)
Getting There: From Hailey, drive north on Main Street (Hwy 75) to Myrtle Street and turn right. Drive up 6 blocks, passing over the bike path and turn left onto Buttercup Road. Drive 2 miles north on Buttercup and park at the junction with Indian Creek on the right.

Miles	The Ride:
0.0	Begin by riding up the paved Indian Creek Road. Stay on the main road.
2.4	Look for a pond on the left side.
3.2	The pavement ends at a circular turn-around. Stay left here along the hillside and the jeep road starts roller-coastering.
3.6	You see a spur road on the left, but continue right on the main trail.
4.6	Gain a small saddle and continue on.
5.3	A spur road to the left climbs to the end of the canyon approximately 3.3 miles away giving great views of the Pioneer Mountains. Stay right and continue on the main trail.
5.5	Begin climbing on and off for the next 2.4 miles.
6.3	Spur road on the right. Continue left on the main road.
6.4	Gain a small saddle and continue on. From here it's pretty much a continuous climb with little resting. Relax and enjoy it, you're almost there!
7.4	Top out on the summit saddle (elev. 7310'). You can either turn around here for a 14.8 mile out and back ride, or continue on down the jeep road toward Quigley Creek. The mileage from here on is the continuation into Quigley Creek.
7.9	Spur road on the right. Continue left on the main trail and through a fence. From here it's a quick, fun downhill. Just stay on the main trail at all times.
10.4	Junction with Quigley Creek. If you were to turn left here, the road would eventually take you into the Quigley Creek to Cove Creek and Slaughterhouse rides. Turn right and down toward Hailey.
16.2	The dirt road ends at the bottom of Quigley Creek. Continue straight for 0.4 mile and turn right at the stop sign onto East Ridge Drive, then take a quick left onto Croy and intersect the bike path on the right just after Sixth Avenue. Ride north 2 miles back to your car.
18.6	Back at your car and the end of the ride.

Indian Creek to Quigley Creek

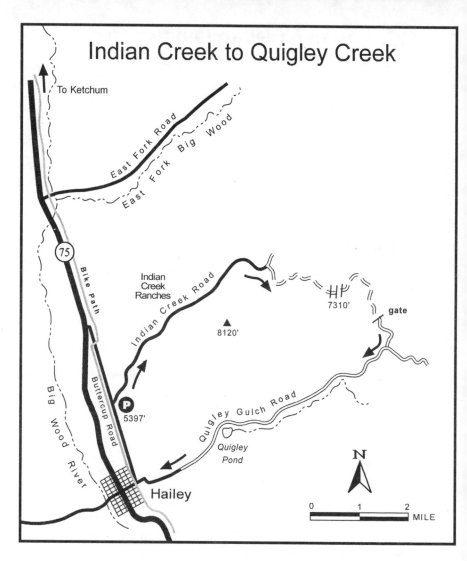

To Ketchum

East Fork Road

East Fork Big Wood

75

Bike Path

Indian Creek Ranches

Indian Creek Road

8120'

7310'

gate

Big Wood River

Buttercup Road

Quigley Gulch Road

5397'

Quigley Pond

N

Hailey

0   1   2   MILE

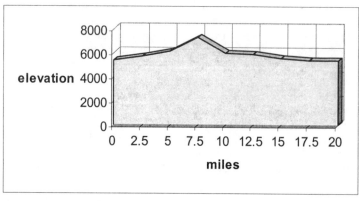

elevation

8000
6000
4000
2000
0

0   2.5   5   7.5   10   12.5   15   17.5   20

miles

13. Ohio Gulch

Length: 14.6 miles
Starting Elevation: 5620'
High Point Elevation: 7870'
Total Elevation Gain: 2250'
The Ride: Out and back
Surface: Dirt jeep road
Difficulty Rating: Moderate/Difficult
Season: Late April - October
Fun Factor: Great views, beautiful canyon setting and a killer pump!
Summary: If you're in the mood for a nice evening or morning pump, this is the ride for you. Beautiful views of the Ohio Gulch Transfer Station (county dump), and the Pioneer and Smoky Mountains.
Getting There: From Ketchum, drive South on Hwy 75 for 6.8 miles and turn left on Ohio Gulch Rd. Immediately park on the right side of the road in the gravel next to the bike path. This is where the ride begins. (*You can also drive up Ohio Gulch Road the 1.8 miles to where the gravel road begins and skip the pavement portion of the ride.)

Miles	The Ride:
0.0	Ride up the paved Ohio Gulch Rd heading toward the foothills.
1.0	The Gun Club appears on the left. Stay on the road toward the transfer station.
1.8	The Transfer station turn off is on the left. Keep straight and continue onto the gravel road which begins weaving around and behind the transfer station. The right fork leads overland to Indian Creek subdivision.
2.9	View point of the upper transfer station and beginning of a quick rocky downhill. At the bottom of the downhill, continue on the main jeep road to the right.
3.2	Gain a small saddle and prepare for some climbing ahead.
3.8	Encounter a small steep hill which is a tough climb.
4.1	Begin a scree-slope hill climb, one of a series to come.
4.3	Gain another small saddle and get ready to climb again.
5.0	The first of a few switchbacks starts here with moderate to easy climbing between them.
5.9	Come into a clearing with awesome views of the Smokey Mountains to the West. Continue up a series of switchbacks and moderate climbing with a steep hill climb to gain the summit saddle.
7.3	The top! Incredible views of the Pioneer Mountains and the canyons of Indian and Quigley creeks. Take some pictures, suck in some air, enjoy the views and get ready for a fast downhill! There is a small single-track leading off to the east which goes around the small knob. It eventually leads down into Indian Creek area.
14.6	End of the ride and (hopefully) back to your car.

Ohio Gulch

To Ketchum

East Fork Road

East Fork Big Wood River

6800'

7870'

7886'

County
Transfer
Station

5520'

Ohio Gulch Road

75

P

N

To Hailey

0   1   2

MILE

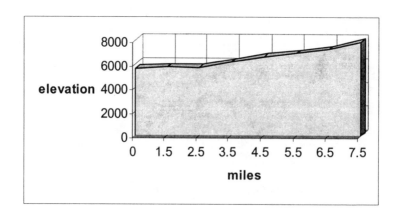

elevation

8000
6000
4000
2000
0

0   1.5   2.5   3.5   4.5   5.5   6.5   7.5

miles

14. North Fork of Deer Creek

Length: 11.3 miles
Starting Elevation: 5970'
High Point Elevation: 7440'
Total Elevation Gain: 1470'
The Ride: Loop
Surface: Dirt jeep road and single track trail
Difficulty Rating: Difficult
Season: Early June - late October
Fun Factor: Beautiful creeks, wildflowers, and high alpine meadows.
Summary: The best part of this ride is getting the climbing done first and having a killer downhill for over 6+ miles. Killer views and tons of wildlife!
Getting There: From Ketchum, drive south on Hwy 75 for 10.9 miles and turn right at the forest service sign for "Deer Creek Road." Follow this road for just over 10 miles to the junction with "North Fork of Deer Creek" and park on the left off the road at this junction. This is where the ride begins.

Miles	The Ride:
0.0	Begin by riding up the N. Fork Deer Creek Road.
1.6	Take the left fork at the trailhead leading up a single track trail.
4.0	The top of the ride at the trail junction. Continue on down the other side toward Poison Flats. The right fork leads to Mars Ridge.
4.4	A small pond is located in the trees here. Not good swimming, but good wildlife viewing possibilities.
4.9	Trail junction. Take the left fork leading down the Deer Creek drainage. The right fork goes toward Poison Flats.
9.0	Pass by Curran Gulch trailhead on the right. Stay on the main trail down.
10.1	Primitive hunting campsite and the start of the jeep road and the end of the single track.
10.7	Pass by the Kinsey Creek trailhead on the right. Stay on the jeep road down.
11.3	You just rode past your car. Hey, hey, turn around, that was the end of the ride.

(This trail is sponsored by WRASTA - Wood River Area Single Track Assoc.)

ULTIMATE
hydration packs to live for

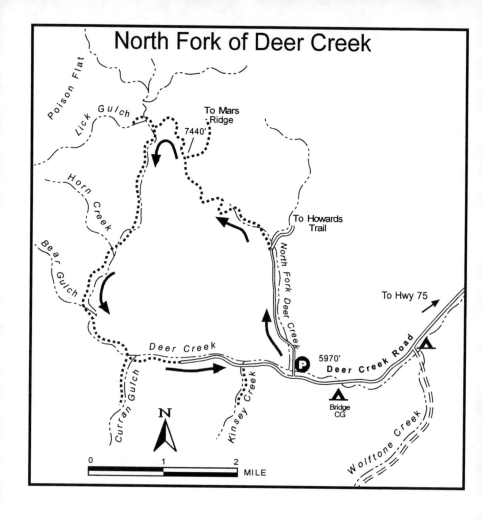

North Fork of Deer Creek

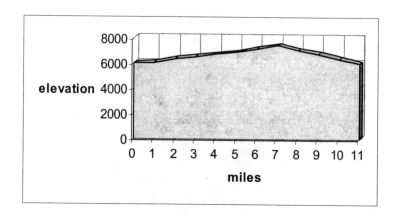

15. Howard's Trail to Mars Ridge

Length: 12.1 miles
Starting Elevation: 6360'
High Point Elevation: 8525'
Total Elevation Gain: 2165'
The Ride: Loop
Surface: Dirt jeep road and single track trail
Difficulty Rating: Difficult/Abusive
Season: June - late October
Fun Factor: 360 degree views of the entire area, wildflowers and a moonscape.
Summary: This is an aerobic ride with some grinding and killer downhills. Bring extra food, water, a jacket and a camera. You'll want and use them all!
Getting There: From Ketchum, drive south on Hwy 75 for 10.9 miles and turn right at the forest service sign for "Deer Creek Road." Follow this road for just over 10 miles to the junction with "North Fork of Deer Creek". Turn right for another 1.6 miles and park on the left near the trailhead sign. This is where the ride begins.

Miles	The Ride:
0.0	Begin by riding up the jeep road following the sign to Howard's Trail.
1.3	The jeep road ends at a small creek crossing. From here it's all single track up the switchbacks to the next junction. All rideable, never too steep.
3.9	The junction with Greenhorn Gulch. Turn left and continue climbing up.
5.0	Another junction at a saddle. Turn left onto and continue more climbing. It gets a bit steeper here and you may have to walk a little bit. Well worth it!
5.7	You are now on the famous Mars Ridge, enjoy the scenery and ride on.
7.3	Now that you're done riding along the ridge, at the junction, turn left and start the descent into the North Fork of Deer Creek.
8.4	An outfitters camp appears on the left.
8.6	You now drop into the trees leaving the upper bowl and ridge behind.
9.8	Junction with North Fork of Deer Creek trail. Turn left (south) and begin an incredibly fun switchback descent (that is if you didn't think the past 2 miles have been a hoot!).
12.1	The single track has ended right at your car. Wow, that was awesome!

Howard's Trail to Mars Ridge

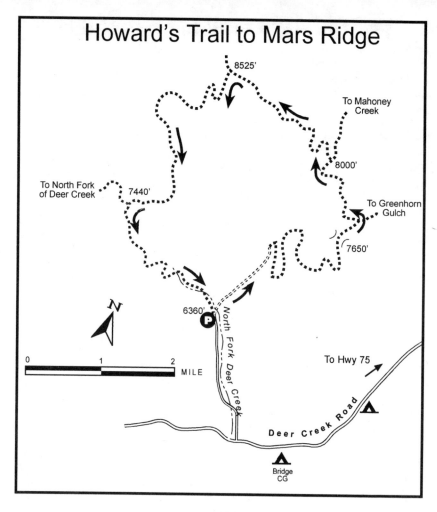

8525'

To Mahoney
Creek

8000'

To North Fork
of Deer Creek

7440'

To Greenhorn
Gulch

7650'

6360'
P

North Fork Deer Creek

N

0   1   2
MILE

To Hwy 75

Deer Creek Road

Bridge
CG

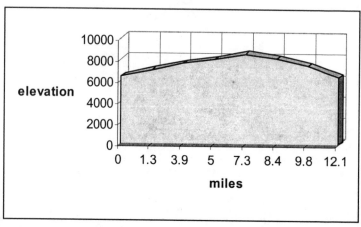

elevation

10000
8000
6000
4000
2000
0

0   1.3   3.9   5   7.3   8.4   9.8   12.1

miles

16. Wolftone Creek to Curran Gulch

Length: 18.4 miles
Starting Elevation: 5850'
High Point Elevation: 7800'
Total Elevation Gain: 1950'
The Ride: Loop
Surface: Dirt jeep road and single track trail
Difficulty Rating: Difficult
Season: June - October
Fun Factor: Views, views and more views.
Summary: This ride rivals any in the area for fun, challenge and views. (*Another option for this ride is to ride to the saddle next to Kelly Mountain and down into Croy Creek. The turn off for that ride is at mile 5 listed below).
Getting There: From Ketchum, drive south on Hwy 75 for approximately 9 miles and turn right at the forest service sign for "Deer Creek Road." Follow this road for just over 8 miles and park on the left by the sign indicating Wolftone Creek.

<u>Miles</u>	<u>The Ride:</u>
0.0	Begin the ride by heading up Wolftone Creek Road.
1.1	After gaining a small hill on mining tailings, follow the road as it turns west and heads up the canyon.
2.7	Spur road and a cabin on the right leads nowhere too exciting. Continue to ride forward.
3.9	End of the road and beginning of single track trail. Continue riding up the valley. DO NOT take the trail which crosses the creek and switches back to the left. Stay right and go straight up the drainage.
4.4	At the fork, stay right. From here the trail crosses the creek several times. Always stay on the main trail.
5.0	Just after a creek crossing you encounter a road going both left and right. Turn right here and begin a pleasant cruise up and through the trees. (*If going to Croy Creek from here, turn left to the Kelly Mountain saddle at the top. Use common sense in directions going down the other side. Its approximately 4.5 miles to Croy Creek Road and 16 miles into Hailey. Use USGS Topo map "Mahoney Butte" and "Richardson Butte").
5.4	After crossing a small creek, continue up the main road. Do not turn left on the faint single track. From here the road is a bit steep and loose.
6.3	The first of many saddles is reached. Follow the road down a bit before starting some serious climbing.
6.8	The road takes a sharp right turn and becomes single track climbing up to the left. You may have to push a bit here, but hang in there. It mellows in a bit before traversing over to the saddle above Kinsey Creek.
8.1	The saddle on top of Kinsey Creek. You can either drop into Kinsey Creek f or a shorter loop, or continue on into Curran Gulch. The details of the rest of this ride are listed on page 42 under the "Kinsey Creek to Curran Gulch" ride #14.

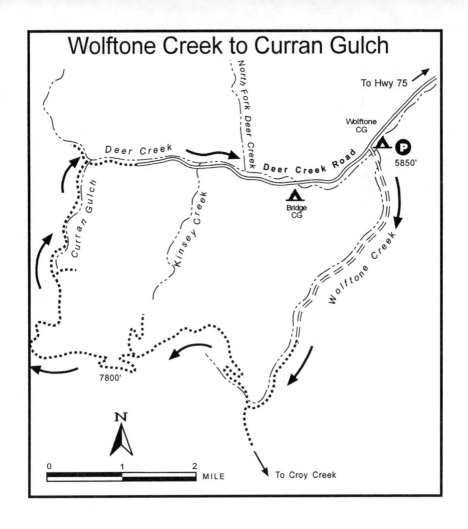

Wolftone Creek to Curran Gulch

To Hwy 75

Wolftone CG

P 5850'

North Fork Deer Creek

Deer Creek

Deer Creek Road

Bridge CG

Curran Gulch

Kinsey Creek

Wolftone Creek

7800'

N

0   1   2 MILE

To Croy Creek

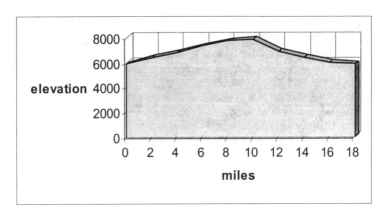

17. Kinsey Creek to Curran Gulch

Length: 10.4 miles
Starting Elevation: 6040'
High Point Elevation: 7800'
Total Elevation Gain: 1760'
The Ride: Loop
Surface: Dirt jeep road and single track trail.
Difficulty Rating: Difficult
Season: Early June - October
Fun Factor: Adventure ride, views, route finding, views, route...
Summary: This isn't as bad as the elevation gain seems, but it is still a grinder. Once up, it's a great run down. Fairly sandy on the way up and technical on the way down. **Some people prefer to do this ride opposite of how it's written here.
Getting There: From Ketchum, drive south on Hwy 75 for approximately 9 miles and turn right at the forest service sign for "Deer Creek Road." Follow this road for 11.5 miles and park next to the unsigned Kinsey Creek coming into the canyon from the left. Park somewhere near by, but please don't block the road.

Miles	The Ride:
0.0	Begin by riding through Deer Creek then up the trail into the Kinsey Creek drainage.
1.2	Pass by a trail leading off to the right which eventually leads into the Curran Gulch drainage. Stay on the main trail passing by a spur road on the left.
1.5	At the fork in the road, take the left and more heavily travelled road which crosses the creek. From here you begin a long climb.
3.5	The top of the saddle. From here the trail gets a bit more interesting. Straight ahead leads into Croy Creek and left leads to Wolftone Creek. Instead, turn right at the top of the saddle and ride for roughly 50+ feet on a primitive trail, before jumping off to the left on a trail which descends quickly to a road about 50 yards below. Yes, it is the trail if you go literally straight down the hill. Turn right onto the road and follow it for one mile, where it starts to switchback to the right and climb.
4.5	After rounding the switchback, continue for a couple hundred yards. Look to your left for a very easy trail to miss leading off to the left traversing the ridge. **DO NOT MISS THIS TURN.
5.5	After gaining the final ridge-top, the trail becomes a bit of a roller-coaster as it drops its way into Curran Gulch.
7.3	You'll come to a trail junction with a trail coming in from Kinsey Creek. Stay straight and continue down the drainage.
8.8	After crossing over Deer Creek, meet up with the Deer Creek Trail and turn right, heading down the drainage.
9.8	Ride past the official trailhead for the Deer Creek Trail and enter into a hunt ers camp and on to a dirt jeep road. Continue down the road.
10.4	The end of the ride and back at the Kinsey Creek trailhead.

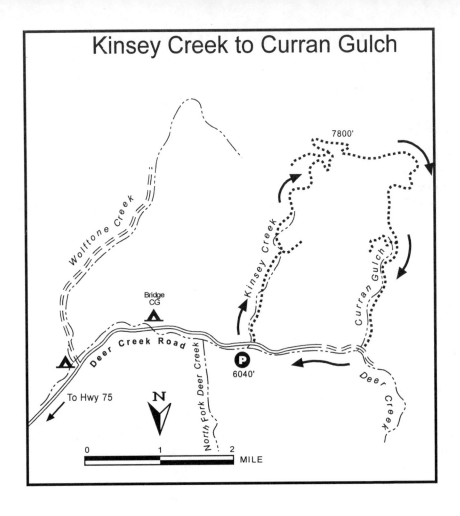

Kinsey Creek to Curran Gulch

7800'

Wolftone Creek

Kinsey Creek

Curran Gulch

Bridge
CG

Deer Creek Road

North Fork Deer Creek

P
6040'

Deer Creek

To Hwy 75

N

0   1   2
MILE

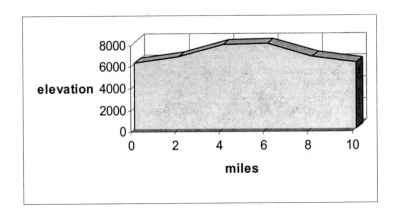

elevation

miles

18. Quigley Creek to Cove Creek

Length: 31.1 miles
Starting Elevation: 5350'
High Point Elevation: 7250'
Total Elevation Gain: 1900'
The Ride: Loop
Surface: Dirt road, single-track, pavement
Difficulty Rating: Moderate/Difficult
Season: Late April - late October

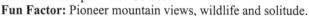

Fun Factor: Pioneer mountain views, wildlife and solitude.

Summary: Whether you shuttle a car to Triumph or make a loop out of it, this is a wonderful ride for most anyone. Due to the length, it will leave you with a good thigh burn. High alpine meadows, aspens and the occasional elk or antelope just add to the experience.

Getting There: From Main Street in Hailey, turn east on Croy Street and follow the road as it takes a natural right turn. Turn left on Quigley Road at the "Deerfield" sign. Follow that street until it joins up with a dirt road heading up the canyon approximately one-half mile later. Park here (For a shorter ride, you may want to shuttle a car to Truimph, up East Fork Canyon. See mile 18.0 on the next page).

Miles	The Ride:
0.0	Begin riding up Quigley Creek Road heading east along side a large field and across the cattle guard.
1.75	Pass the Quigley Pond on the right side of the road.
2.2	Small spur road on the right, continue straight on Quigley Creek Road.
2.5	The spur road rejoins the main road.
4.2	Pass a corral then a spur road just a bit further on the left side.
5.8	Spur road on the left leads to/from Indian Creek. Continue up the main road curving to the south up and through some clear cuts. Always stay on the main road through this area.
7.6	Small private cabin appears off to the right.
7.7	Spur road and switchback leads off to the right which heads over and down to Slaughterhouse Creek and into Bellevue. Instead stay on the main road cross ing over a small creek bed (possibly dry in mid to late summer) and heading northeast.
8.6	Saddle in a mud bog area. Take the first left heading down the canyon to the northeast and left. Do not turn right, it leads nowhere.
9.1	After a bit of a rutted downhill, a road takes off to the left just before a muddy creek crossing. Stay on the main road through the muddy crossing.
9.4	Take a left on the grassy double-track . . . trust me.
10.1	Take another left and go down the hill.
10.4	Yes, go left again and begin the famous Narrows single-track trail.
11.7	The Narrows ends at the Cove Creek Road. Go right and toward the beaver' ponds, heading north.
12.6	A fun descent leads to a junction with another main road. Go right here passing by the beaver ponds and a spur road on the right. Continue on down the main road.
13.7	Pass by Hook Draw on the right.
14.2	Small spur road on the left leads to nowhere.

16.2	Major junction here. This is East Fork Road. Turn left here.
17.2	Spur road off to the right leads to Hyndman Creek and the Pioneer Mountains main "peak" district.
18.5	Pavement and the town of Triumph. If you shuttled a car here, this is the end of your ride. If you're bumming there's no car here, continue down the paved East Fork Road.
24.4	Turn left before Hwy 75 and head south on the paved bike path.
30.6	As the bike path comes into Hailey, follow it to Croy Street and turn left here retracing your route back to your car.
31.1	Back at your car at Quigley Canyon and the end of the ride.

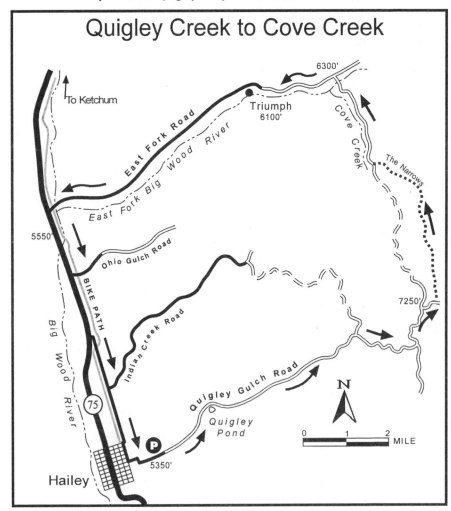

Quigley Creek to Cove Creek

19. Hyndman Creek Road

Length: 12 miles
Starting Elevation: 6100'
High Point Elevation: 7000'
Total Elevation Gain: 900'
The Ride: Out and back
Surface: Dirt jeep road
Difficulty Rating: Easy/Moderate
Season: May - October
Fun Factor: Pioneer Mountain views, high alpine meadows and wildlife.
Summary: This ride is the "mountain vistas" ride if there ever was one. Hyndman Creek and the majestic Pioneer Mountains with the occasional elk and deer add to the experience.
Getting There: From Ketchum, drive south on Hwy 75 to East Fork Road, approximately 5 miles. Turn left (east) here and drive approximately 6 miles to the tiny town of Triumph and park on the eastern most edge of town where gravel meets the pavement. Please park far enough off the side of the road so local residents don't have to veer around your car.

Miles	The Ride:
0.0	Begin riding east on the main road away from Triumph.
0.4	Cross over Hyndman Creek (bridge).
1.2	Turn left onto Hyndman Creek Road #203, which is a very short, steep and rocky road that quickly slacks off to a level gravel cruiser. Along this next stretch, there are many spur roads off to the left leading toward the creek with primitive campsites everywhere.
3.5	At the small fork, turn left and down towards Hyndman Creek. The right fork leads to a private residence, don't go there.
3.6	Cross over the bridge and Hyndman Creek continuing on the main road. All of the land on both sides of the road is private so please respect the landowners privacy and cruise through this short section.
4.1	Spur road on the left leads to Bear Gulch Trail #121 and eventually into Elkhorn if you're a bit adventurous. If not, continue forward on the main road.
4.4	A very large meadow has a tennis court on the right and an old miners cabin on the left. A short bit later at the fork, turn left.
4.5	Spur road on the left leads to Johnstone Creek Trail #206. Continue on the main road.
6.0	This is the end of the ride at the trailhead of North Fork Hyndman Creek Trail #121. From here you can continue on down the canyon and back to your car. Or be a bit adventurous and continue up trail #121 for about 3 miles before it becomes rather steep for biking and switchbacks up to Pioneer Cabin at 9440'. It is a very enjoyable continuation.
12.0	The end of the ride and back at your car.

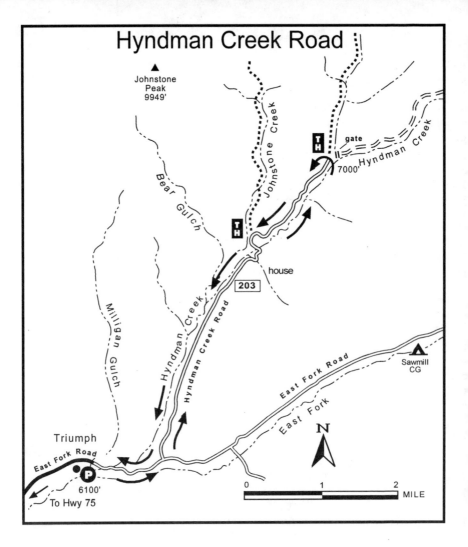

Hyndman Creek Road

Johnstone
Peak
9949'

Johnstone Creek

gate

7000' Hyndman Creek

TH

Bear Gulch

house

203

Milligan Gulch

Hyndman Creek

Hyndman Creek Road

East Fork Road

Sawmill
CG

East Fork

N

Triumph

East Fork Road

P

6100'

To Hwy 75

0   1   2

MILE

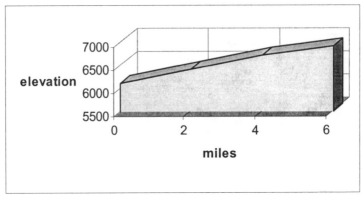

elevation

7000
6500
6000
5500

0   2   4   6

miles

20. Parker to Bear Gulch Loop

Length: 20.8 miles
Starting Elevation: 6005"
High Point Elevation: 8610"
Total Elevation Gain: 2605'
The Ride: Loop
Surface: Dirt jeep road and single track
Difficulty Rating: Difficult
Season: Late-May - October
Fun Factor: Pioneer Mountain views like you've never seen before.
Summary: You'll burn your lungs and pound your legs, all for the most amazing views and wildlife everywhere! This is a must-do ride if ya think ya can handle it!
Getting There: From Ketchum, drive south on Hwy 75 to East Fork Road, approximately 5 miles. Turn left (east) here and drive approximately 5 miles and park on the left where a major dirt jeep road takes off. This is where the ride begins. If you went to Triumph, turn around 1 mile to the starting point.

Miles	**The Ride:**
0.0	Begin by riding up Triumph Gulch on a fairly major jeep road.
1.5	At the fork, stay left here.
2.9	Round a saddle with views of Elkhorn and the valley below.
4.2	Go screaming by Independence Mine. DO NOT GO INTO ANY SHAFTS!
5.5	Jeep road ends at pavement above The Ranch at Elkhorn condos.
6.1	At the stop sign, go right.
6.7	Again, at the stop sign go right. This is the beginning of Parker Gulch Road.
8.5	The gravel road now becomes double track jeep road.
9.4	In the big grassy meadow, stay left and you'll find the trail again. It is single track from here on up.
9.9	The switchbacks begin. Now is when you need those lungs and legs!
11.4	The first saddle, hold on, there's more...
12.0	The top of the ride at 8610', overlooking Uncle John's Gulch to the north and Bear Gulch to the south. To the east are the Pioneer Mountains.
12.5	A small saddle before really dropping into Bear Gulch. Stay left at the fork.
15.5	Single track ends at a double track jeep road.
15.7	Junction with Hydeman Creek Road, stay right and down. You'll follow this all the way down the valley.
18.6	Take a right onto East Fork Road.
19.8	The town of Triumph. Watch for kids and cruise through town.
20.8	Back at your car and the end of another awesome ride!

Parker-Bear Gulch Loop

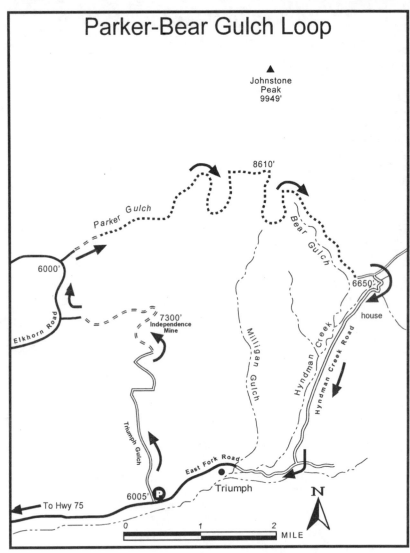

Johnstone Peak 9949'

8610'

Parker Gulch

6000'

Elkhorn Road

7300'
Independence Mine

Bear Gulch

6650'

house

Milligan Gulch

Hyndman Creek

Hyndman Creek Road

Triumph Gulch

East Fork Road

Triumph

6005' P

To Hwy 75

N

0   1   2   MILE

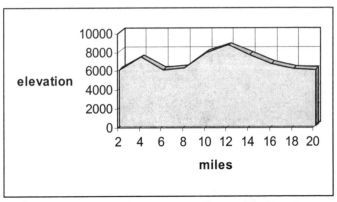

elevation

10000
8000
6000
4000
2000
0

2 4 6 8 10 12 14 16 18 20

miles

Ketchum, Idaho, circa 1910
courtesy of Wood River Journal

"They want'd t' call th' town Leadville, but th' govrn'mt said there was too many already. So they settled for Ketchum and I'm right proud they did. After all, I built th' first cabin here back in '79 . . . Course th' way th' silver's runnin' out, might not matter what th' town's name is anyhow. Folks is already headin' for th' new boomtowns. Heck, we got more dogs than people now days. . . Wonder what'll happen t' ol' Ketchum. Prob'ly dry up and blow away . . . "

> Dave Ketchum
> Circa 1890
> Trapper, Mountain Man

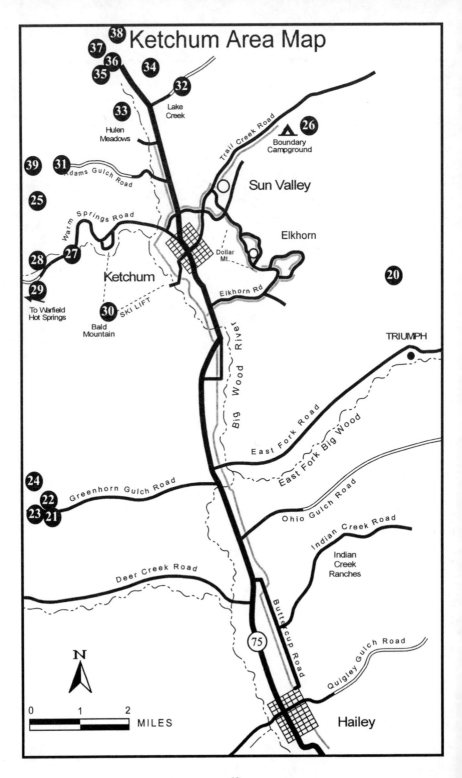

Ketchum Area Map

Lake Creek

Trail Creek Road

Hulen Meadows

Boundary Campground

Sun Valley

Adams Gulch Road

Warm Springs Road

Elkhorn

Ketchum

Dollar Mt.

To Warfield Hot Springs

SKI LIFT

Bald Mountain

Elkhorn Rd

Big Wood River

TRIUMPH

East Fork Road

East Fork Big Wood

Greenhorn Gulch Road

Ohio Gulch Road

Indian Creek Road

Indian Creek Ranches

Deer Creek Road

Buttercup Road

Quigley Gulch Road

N

0   1   2   MILES

75

Hailey

60

21. Imperial Gulch

Length: 10.5 miles
Starting Elevation: 5900'
High Point Elevation: 7450'
Total Elevation Gain: 1550'
The Ride: Loop
Surface: Single track trail
Difficulty Rating: Moderate/Difficult
Season: May - October
Fun Factor: Scenic, fun loop and incredible downhill.
Summary: With a grind up Greenhorn Gulch, you are rewarded with a great descent into Imperial Gulch with views, flowers, wildlife and more views.
Getting There: From Ketchum, drive south on Hwy 75 for 6 miles and turn west (right) onto Greenhorn Gulch Road. Drive 3.8 miles up the road to the parking lot. The ride begins here.

<u>Miles</u>	<u>The Ride:</u>
0.0	Follow the trail exiting the parking lot area on the west side. The beginning of this trail is quite rocky and rough, but don't let this turn you off, it becomes great at the top.
1.0	Pass by Cow Creek Trail on the right.
1.4	Trail junction: Right trail leads to Mahoney Creek and Lodgepole Creek, but turn left and continue up toward Deer Creek, gradually climbing through pines next to the stream.
3.8	You see an unsigned trail on the right leads up Mahoney Creek, but continue straight on the main trail heading toward Deer Creek with casual climbing through beautiful pines alongside the creek.
4.9	You encounter a trail junction at the saddle. From here take a hard left, passing by a trail exiting off to the right and down into Deer Creek. This is the beginning of Imperial Gulch Trail. For the next 2.7 miles the trail traverses with minimal climbing giving wonderful views of Deer Creek and the Mahoney Creek drainages.
7.6	Whoa! Be sure and turn right here where the sign indicates "trail."
8.1	Faint trail leading off to the right leads into Deer Creek. Stay straight on the main trail heading down the gulch.
8.8	Trail junction at the fence. The right trail leads to another Imperial Gulch trailhead. Instead, turn left, traversing gradually up and to a saddle overlooking Greenhorn Gulch.
9.3	The saddle. Continue on down the trail.
10.3	The bottom of the Imperial Gulch Trail at the intersection with Greenhorn Gulch. Turn right and continue back to the trailhead.
10.5	The end of the ride and back at the trailhead.

(This trail is sponsored by Base Mountain Properties)

Imperial Gulch

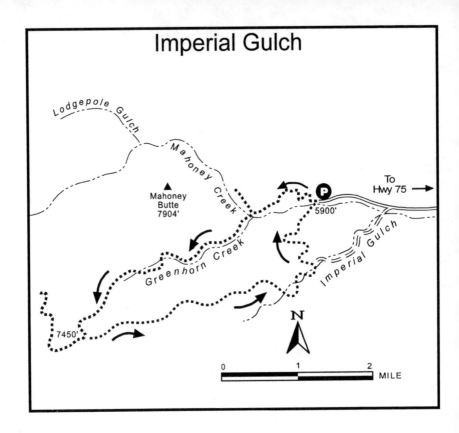

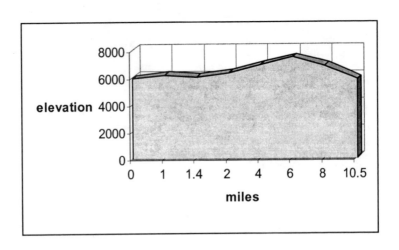

22. Lodgepole Gulch

Length: 11.9 miles
Starting Elevation: 5900'
High Point Elevation: 7850'
Total Elevation Gain: 1950'
The Ride: Loop
Surface: Single track trail
Difficulty Rating: Moderate/Difficult
Season: May - late October
Fun Factor: Wildflowers, climbing, great downhill, meadows.
Summary: This whole area is a great place for riding, no matter which loop you do. Lodgepole Gulch is known for its great downhills and moderate climbs.
Getting There: From Ketchum, drive south on Hwy 75 for 6 miles and turn west (right) onto Greenhorn Gulch Road. Drive 3.8 miles up the road to the parking lot. The ride begins here.

Miles	The Ride:
0.0	Follow the trail exiting the parking lot area on the west side. The beginning of this trail is quite rocky and rough, but don't let this turn you off.
1.0	Pass by Cow Creek Trail on the right.
1.4	Trail junction: Turn right toward Mahoney Creek Trail and Lodgepole Trail and begin a gradual ascent.
3.7	You reach a trail junction. Turn right and into Lodgepole Gulch. From here you climb about 1000' feet over the next 2.1 miles. It is never too hard, so take many deep breaths, endure the grind and relax and enjoy the beautiful scenes.
5.8	Trail junction at the top of Lodgepole Gulch. Turn left and begin descending down into Mahoney Creek. The right trail leads into Red Warrior Creek.
6.7	Trail junction: The right fork leads to the top of Mahoney Creek, instead, turn left and down the drainage.
8.4	Trail junction: The left fork leads back up into Lodgepole Gulch, instead, turn right and down heading back to the trailhead.
10.5	Trail junction: The right fork leads up Greenhorn Gulch and into Deer Creek. Instead, turn left to complete the loop.
11.9	The end of the ride and back at the trailhead.

Lodgepole Gulch

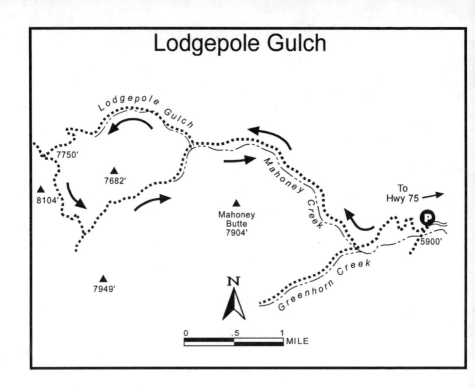

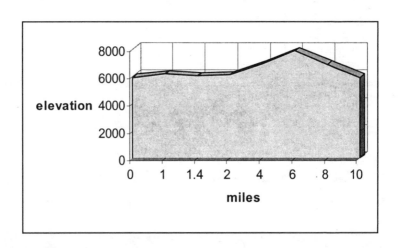

23. Greenhorn Gulch to Mahoney Creek

Length: 12.8 miles
Starting Elevation: 5900'
High Point Elevation: 8000'
Total Elevation Gain: 2100'
The Ride: Loop
Surface: Single track trail
Difficulty Rating: Difficult
Season: May - late October
Fun Factor: Moderate climbs leading to excellent views and downhills.
Summary: This ride is always an aerobic challenge with wonderful single track trails, views of the Pioneer mountains and some of the best downhill riding around.
Getting There: From Ketchum, drive south on Hwy 75 for 6 miles and turn west (right) onto Greenhorn Gulch Road. Drive 3.8 miles up the road to the parking lot. The ride begins here.

<u>Miles</u>	<u>The Ride:</u>
0.0	Follow the trail exiting the parking lot area on the west side. The beginning of this trail is quite rocky and rough, but don't let this turn you off.
1.0	Pass by Cow Creek Trail on the right.
1.4	Trail junction: Right trail leads to Mahoney Creek and Lodgepole Creek, but turn left and continue up toward "Deer Creek," ascending the trail through pines next to a stream.
3.8	An unsigned trail on the right leads up Mahoney Creek, continue straight on the main trail heading toward Deer Creek.
4.9	Catch your breath at the trail junction midway through the climb. Hard left eventually leads to Imperial Gulch Trail #155, while a soft left leads down a jeep trail to Deer Creek via Panther Creek. Instead, continue grinding up and right on Mahoney Creek Trail #156 climbing a few switchbacks eventually gaining the top of the ride with incredible views of the Pioneer mountains to the east.
6.6	After a few roller-coasters, you come to a trail junction. Left trail leads down Red Warrior Creek Trail #152, but continue down right on the main trail eventually passing by the unsigned Mahoney Creek trail in a saddle on the right side after 0.5 miles.
7.6	Trail junction: Left trail leads into Lodgepole Creek. Instead, continue down and right on the main trail through a wonderful tree slalom course. Please remember your trail etiquette here, no skidding and yield to all others.
9.1	Trail junction: Left trail leads up Lodgepole Creek. Continue the ride down on the main trail. Watch that smile, you may have to pick a few bugs out of your teeth.
11.4	The loop is complete. Continue left and down crossing the stream two more times, the same way you came up.
12.8	End of the ride at the parking lot.

(This trail is sponsored by Formula Sports)

Greenhorn Gulch to Mahoney

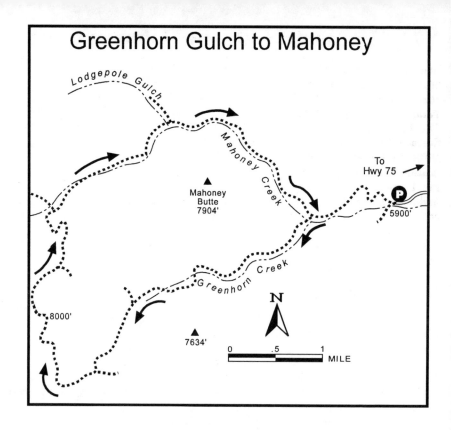

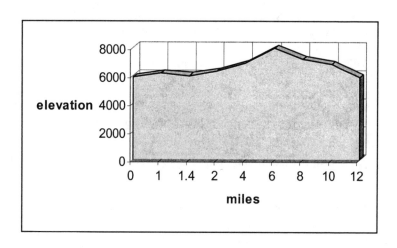

24. Red Warrior Creek

Length: 10.7 miles (30.2 miles for Loop)
Starting Elevation: 5900'
High Point Elevation: 7850'
Total Elevation Gain: 1950'
The Ride: One-way
Surface: Single track trail and dirt jeep road
Difficulty Rating: Difficult
Season: May - late October
Fun Factor: Great climbing, killer descent and hot springs.
Summary: A ride up Lodgepole Gulch leads to a great technical descent through creeks and rocks to a huge creek crossing and hot springs. Views abound in every direction.
Getting There: From Ketchum, drive south on Hwy 75 for 6 miles and turn west (right) onto Greenhorn Gulch Road. Drive 3.8 miles up the road to the parking lot. The ride begins here. **You may want to shuttle a car up Warm Springs Road to the end of the ride at Warfield Hot Springs, or plan on enjoying the casual ride back down Warm Springs Road into Ketchum and back to the trailhead (approx. 20 miles).

Miles	**The Ride:**
0.0	Follow the trail exiting the parking lot area on the west side. The trail is quite rocky and rough, but don't let this turn you off, it becomes great at the top.
1.0	Pass by Cow Creek Trail on the right.
1.4	Trail junction: Turn right toward Mahoney Creek Trail and Lodgepole Trail and begin a gradual ascent.
3.7	You reach a trail junction. Turn right and into Lodgepole Gulch. From here you climb about 1000' feet over the next 2.1 miles. It is never too hard, so take many deep breaths, endure the grind and relax and enjoy the beautiful scenes.
5.8	At the next trail junction, turn right heading up and over into Red Warrior Creek. The left fork here drops down into Mahoney Creek.
6.1	At the saddle between Lodgepole Gulch and Red Warrior Creek, you begin some fast descending switchbacks for the next 1.2 miles. Once at the bottom and into the Red Warrior Creek drainage, prepare to get wet. You'll cross the creek anywhere between 16 and 24 times, depending upon the time of year and dryness of the upper creek.
8.3	Continuing forward, you'll pass by a trail leading up and to the left. That trail eventually joins up to Mars Ridge.
9.2	Prepare for a gnarly descent. Soon you'll notice an old metal shack and from here the trail crosses the creek 8 times while the trail winds its way down the drainage.
10.7	The climax of the ride . . . crossing over Warm Springs Creek. No, there is not a bridge, so get wet and enjoy it. This is the end of the ride if you shuttled a car to this point. Warm Springs Road is right in front of you, as are about three hot-springs next to the creek a couple hundred yards down the road. Turn right, and from here it is approximately ten miles back to Ketchum, and an additional ten miles back to the Greenhorn Gulch Trailhead, all gradually descending.

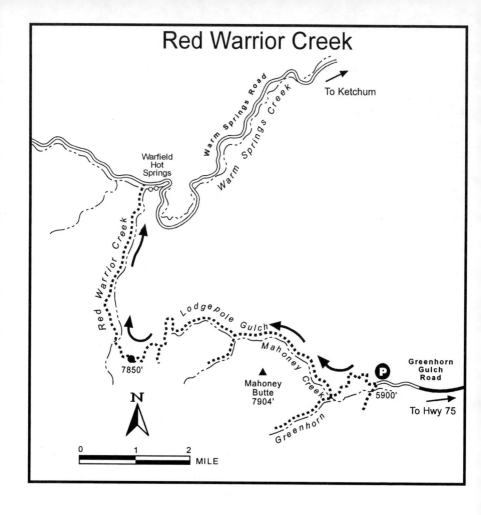

Red Warrior Creek

Warm Springs Road

Warm Springs Creek

To Ketchum

Warfield Hot Springs

Red Warrior Creek

Lodgepole Gulch

Mahoney Creek

7850'

Mahoney Butte 7904'

Greenhorn Gulch Road

P

5900'

To Hwy 75

Greenhorn

N

0   1   2
MILE

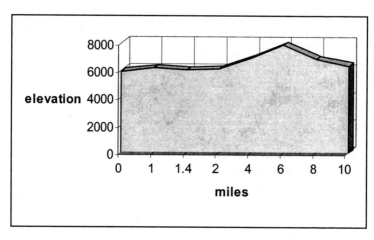

25. Eve Gulch

Length: 14.5 miles
Starting Elevation: 5600'
High Point Elevation: 7900'
Total Elevation Gain: 2300'
The Ride: Loop
Surface: Pavement, dirt jeep road and single track trail
Difficulty Rating: Abusive
Season: May - late October
Fun Factor: Incredible views of three mountain ranges, wildlife, wildflowers.
Summary: This is certainly not a first date ride. However, if you are an abusive rider, then this ride has your name all over it. Endless steep climbing and rocky downhills will be your entertainment. **Some people like to do this ride opposite of how it's written here.
Getting There: From Ketchum, drive north on Hwy 75 for 3 blocks and turn left at the light and onto Warm Springs Road. Drive 1/2 mile further to the corner of Warm Springs Road and Saddle Road. Park in the parking lot of the Park & Ride lot (big vacant lot) on the east side (right side) of the road to begin the ride, or park anywhere close by.

Miles	The Ride:
0.0	Begin by crossing the bridge over the Big Wood River and riding west up Warm Springs Road. Be careful, this is a busy road.
1.6	Four way stop sign. Left road leads to the shops of Warm Springs area and the ski area. Continue forward through the stop sign and up the main road.
3.0	Pass Penny Lake on the left side of the road.
4.1	Pavement ends and an oiled dirt road takes over.
5.7	Whoa! Turn right here at the West Fork Warm Springs Creek (Eve Gulch) trail #146. This is where the fun begins and the climbing stops . . . or is it the other way around?
6.8	After passing by Moonlight Gulch, the road forks at two canyons. Take the right fork.
7.3	The road takes a sharp right turn and starts a grueling climb up the side of the mountain, continually steep at times. Hey, good for the heart, huh?
8.0	After the road makes a sharp left on a switchback onto the ridge, look for a small cairn off to the right side of the road leading to the single-track trail after about a hundred yards (note: the single track trail is before the very steep road in front of you).
8.6	After traversing across the mountainside and through the pinetrees, you encounter an old mining camp.
8.8	At last, the top of Eve Gulch. Catch your breath and check out the 360 degree views of the Smoky, Boulder and Pioneer Mountains. Follow the trail to the right and down into Eve Gulch. Be careful here, the trail can be quite rutted and loose at times.
10.0	The single-track becomes a double-track jeep trail.
11.0	Junction with Adams Gulch Road #141. Turn right here and continue down the jeep road, or abuse yourself further and do the Adams Gulch Loop.
11.4	Turn right onto Shadyside Trail #177A, a single-track trail which contours the hillside above Adams Gulch on the south side of the canyon.

12.9 At the end of Shadyside Trail, turn right and up the hill on the rather wide trail known as "Heidelberg Hill." After gaining the saddle a short distance later, continue down the drainage either on the jeep trail or the single-track on the left side. No more climbing, we promise.

13.7 End of the dirt trail and the beginning of the pavement. Turn left here on Hillside then an immediate right onto Wanderer. At the intersection with Warm Springs Road, turn left and continue back to your car at the Park-n-Ride lot area.

14.5 End of the ride and back at your car. Whew! Where's the PowerTarts?!

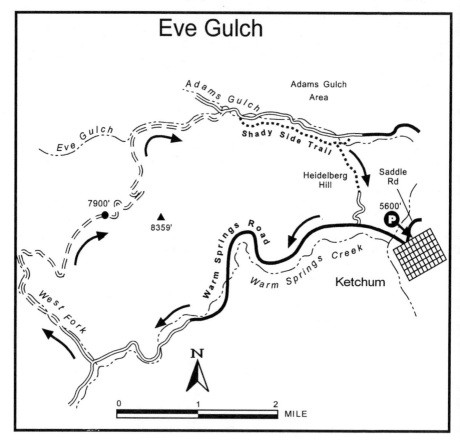

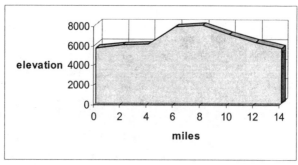

26. Corral Creek

Length: 6.8 miles
Starting Elevation: 6075'
High Point: 6750'
Elevation Gain: 675'
Type of Ride: Out & back
Ride Surface: Single track trail
Difficulty: Easy/Moderate
Riding Season: Late April - late October
Fun Factor: Sagebrush slalom courses with incredible downhills. It is the classic ride.
Summary: This ride has it all, quick climbs (never too steep), quick turns in a slalom fashion, and one of the best downhills this close to Ketchum. Even though this is an out & back ride, it is totally different and enjoyable each way.
Getting There: From Ketchum, drive east on Sun Valley/Trail Creek Road for 3.7 miles, passing by Trail Creek Cabin along the way. Turn right where the sign points to Trail Creek Trailhead, just past the Boundary Campground. Besure to park in the trailhead parking lot and NOT the picnic or campground areas. The ride begins here. (*please note that this is a new trailhead starting mid-summer 2001, the old trailhead was located behind Trail Creek Cabin. Please do not use the old trailhead.)

Miles	The Ride:
0.0	Begin by riding down the gravel trail through the campground and across the bridge. Follow this trail up the embankment to the trail junction.
0.1	Trail junction. Turn left and follow the single track trail along the foothills heading up the valley. Remember to stay on single track the entire time, since you will be crossing a few faint jeep roads along the way.
1.4	Whoa! Trail junction. Stay to the right on the main trail. The left fork leads down to Trail Creek Road.
2.9	Junction with a jeep road crossing. Simply cross the road and keep cruising!
3.4	Take a minute, unpack your lunch or just enjoy Uncle Johns Gulch and the sheep corrals. From here turn around and get ready for the best ride of your life.
6.8	End of the ride and return to Trail Creek Trailhead parking lot.

(This trail is sponsored by Jytte Mau Designs)

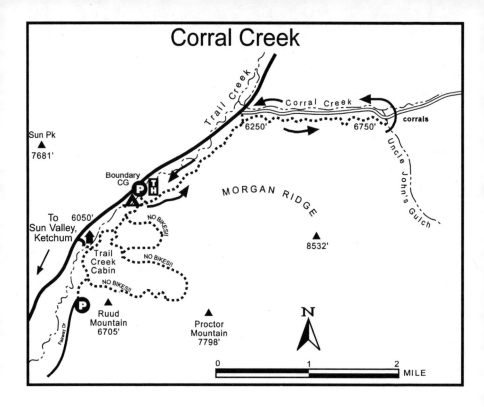

Corral Creek

Trail Creek

Corral Creek

6250' 6750'

corrals

Uncle John's Gulch

Sun Pk
7681'

Boundary CG

MORGAN RIDGE

8532'

To Sun Valley, Ketchum

6050'

NO BIKES!!

Trail Creek Cabin

NO BIKES!!

NO BIKES!!

P

Ruud Mountain
6705'

Proctor Mountain
7798'

Fairway Dr

N

| 0 | 1 | 2 |
MILE

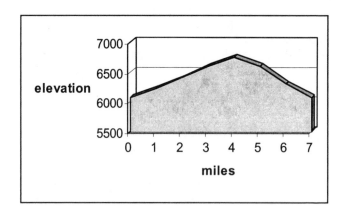

elevation

7000
6500
6000
5500

0 1 2 3 4 5 6 7

miles

27. Warm Springs Road

Length: 48 miles (24 miles from Warfield Hot Springs).
Starting Elevation: 5600'
High Point Elevation: 8719'
Total Elevation Gain: 3119'
The Ride: Out and back
Surface: Pavement and dirt jeep road
Difficulty Rating: Easy/Moderate (Difficult for the last 6.4 miles)
Season: Mid-April to late October.
Fun Factor: Great cruiser in a beautiful mountainous setting.
Summary: Not everyone is in the mood for a hard-core ride all the time, and if you're not, this is the one for you. If you ride to the junction of Middle/South forks of Warm Springs Creek, it is just over 1200 ft of vertical in 17.6 miles . . . not too bad.
Getting There: From Ketchum, drive north on Hwy 75 for 3 blocks and turn left at the light and onto Warm Springs Road. Drive 1/2 mile further to the corner of Warm Springs Road and Saddle Road. Park in the parking lot of the Park & Ride lot on the East side of the road to begin the ride, or drive up Warm Springs Creek Road to Warfield Hot Springs (10 miles) for an alternate starting point.

Miles	The Ride:
0.0	Ride up Warm Springs Creek Road.
1.6	Stop sign. Continue forward through the stop sign and up the road.
3.0	Pass by the very small Penny Lake on the left side of the road.
4.1	Here the pavement ends and the dirt road takes over.
5.7	The West Fork of Warm Springs Creek (Eve Gulch) trail takes off on right.
10.0	Warfield Hot Springs. Here there are natural hot springs to soak in next to the creek, a small cliff to top-rope climb on and the trailhead to Red Warrior Creek ride.
11.6	Rooks Creek takes off on the right. Trust us, don't go here.
12.7	Thompson Creek road on the right. Keep going on the main road.
14.3	Barr Gulch road on the right. Not this way please.
15.3	Pass by Castle Creek Trail #140 on the right side. Adventurous? yes.
16.7	Pass by Placer Creek Road #162 on the right by the sheep paddocks.
17.6	Road #046 takes off to the left leading to the Middle and South forks of Warm Springs Creek. Either turn around here or get ready to climb continually up a grinding but never too relentless road. This is where the moderate part of the ride starts.
24.0	Dollarhide Summit elevation 8719' with wonderful views of the Pioneer and Smokey mountains. Now get ready for an incredible downhill for 24 miles back to Ketchum! Or keep going on these backroads all the way to Boise!

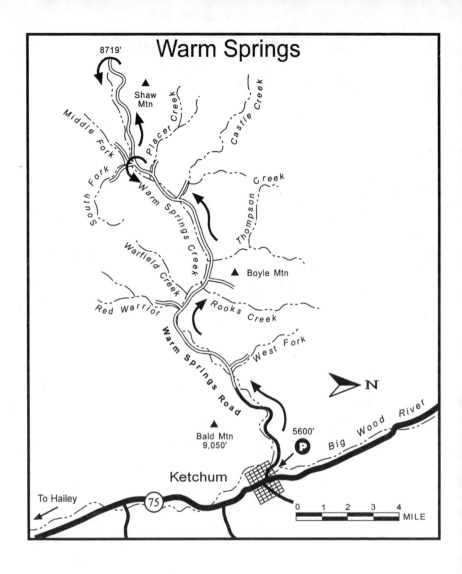

Warm Springs

8719'

Shaw Mtn

Middle Fork

South Fork

Placer Creek

Castle Creek

Thompson Creek

Warm Springs Creek

Warfield Creek

Boyle Mtn

Red Warrior

Rooks Creek

West Fork

Warm Springs Road

N

Bald Mtn
9,050'

5600'

P

Big Wood River

Ketchum

To Hailey

75

| 0 | 1 | 2 | 3 | 4 |

MILE

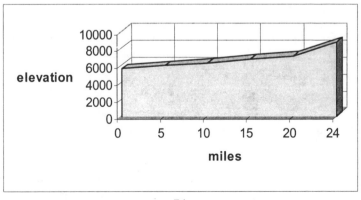

elevation

10000
8000
6000
4000
2000
0

0   5   10   15   20   24

miles

28. Placer Creek to Castle Creek

Length: 10.9 miles
Starting Elevation: 6640'
High Point Elevation: 8220'
Total Elevation Gain: 1580'
The Ride: Loop
Surface: Dirt jeep road and single track
Difficulty Rating: Moderate/Difficult
Season: Late May to October
Fun Factor: Adventure and the feeling of being way out there.
Summary: If you can get by the loose rock and pushing for a little ways on the way up, you'll dig the downhill all the way back to your car.
Getting There: From Ketchum, drive north on Hwy 75 for 3 blocks and turn left at the light and onto Warm Springs Road. Follow this road for approximately 15.5 miles and park on the left just after the trailhead sign for Castle Creek. You'll know you're there when a big castle-like rock appears on the north side of the creek. This is where the ride begins.

Miles	The Ride:
0.0	Begin by riding up Warm Springs Road to the turn off for Placer Creek.
1.3	Turn right on the jeep road next to the corrals. Stay on this main road.
2.3	Cross the obvious creek in front of you.
3.0	Another creek crossing . . . enjoy the wetness!
3.1	This rough road leads to a small sign on the right. Follow the trail to the right.
4.8	Stay on the main trail here.
5.0	The trail starts to level out a bit and then hits a very marshy area. It's not that bad, and the upper end of the water crested stream has some small logs to cross on. From here follow the trail through the forest where it goes through numerous springs and over logs. Eventually it dries out.
5.5	The top of the ride. Get ready for the most amazing downhill. Be careful!
6.6	After some serious switchbacks, you cross over Castle Creek. Go right.
8.3	Cross over the North Fork of Castle Creek. Look upstream for a crossing.
9.5	The trail goes through a huge meadow and disappears. Stay straight through the meadow and the trail reappears at the other end.
10.7	Cross through Castle Creek. Get wet, you're almost done!
10.8	Cross through Warm Springs Creek. Keep trying until you get it. Get wet!
10.9	After crossing Warm Springs Creek, turn right on the road and to your car.

(This trail sponsored by WRASTA - Wood River Area Single Track Association)

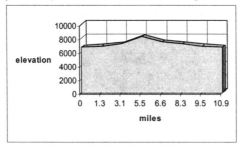

Placer Creek to Castle Creek

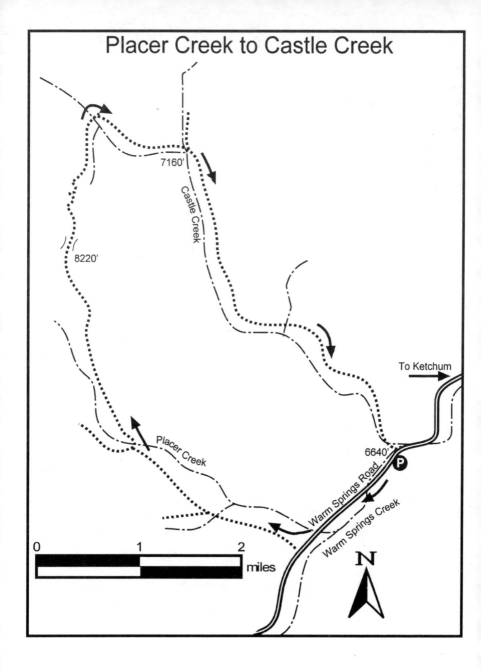

7160'

Castle Creek

8220'

To Ketchum

Placer Creek

6640'

Warm Springs Road

Warm Springs Creek

N

0   1   2
miles

29. Poison Flat Trail

Length: 13.2 miles
Starting Elevation: 6850'
High Point Elevation: 7900'
Total Elevation Gain: 1050'
The Ride: One-way
Surface: Dirt jeep road and single track trail
Difficulty Rating: Difficult
Season: Late May - late October
Fun Factor: Wildflowers, high alpine meadows, cruiser downhills.
Summary: Moderate climbing, great views and incredible downhills
Getting There: From the heart of Ketchum, drive north on Hwy 75 for 3 blocks and turn left onto Warm Springs Road. Follow this road up Warm Springs Canyon approximately 18 miles where a pull-out on the left shows signs for Road #046 (South and Middle Forks of Warm Springs Creek). Park anywhere near here. You will need to shuttle a car to the North Fork of Deer Creek parking area (see the North Fork of Deer Creek ride #12 on page 38 for directions).

Miles	The Ride:
0.0	Begin by riding up the South Fork of Warm Springs #046 in a southerly direction on a partial jeep road, immediately forging a stream.
0.7	Turn left at the sign for Meadow Creek Trail and cross the creek.
1.0	Again, turn left at the sign for South Fork of Warm Springs Trail #151.
2.4	Trail junction: The left fork goes up to Red Warrior Creek. Instead, go right and continue up the South Fork of Warm Springs Trail #199.
3.1	The trail turns into a tough climb up through loose scree for only a short distance, gaining a small saddle soon thereafter.
4.3	Trail junction: Do not go right, it is a very challenging trail which could involve a few tears and hair pulling. Instead, save the marriage and turn left onto the Poison Flat Trail #218 and begin a scenic cruise across the high alpine sage-brush meadow.
6.6	Trail junction: The left fork goes up and over into the North Fork of Deer Creek. Take the right fork into the main drainage of Deer Creek. However, either trail will get you back to your (shuttled) car at the trailhead.
8.7	As you descend, pass by Horn Creek on the right and a mile later is Bear Gulch.
10.7	Pass by Curran Gulch on the right side.
12.0	The trailhead for Deer Creek Trail and a primitive hunters camp. Continue on down the main jeep road.
13.2	The end of the ride and back at your car.

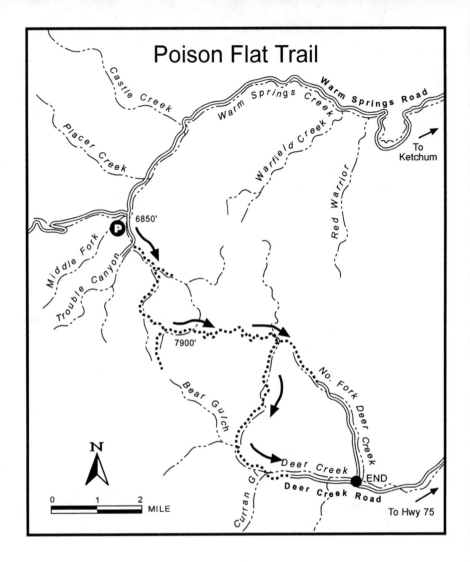

Poison Flat Trail

Castle Creek

Placer Creek

Warm Springs Creek

Warm Springs Road

To Ketchum

Warfield Creek

Red Warrior

Middle Fork

Trouble Canyon

P 6850'

7900'

Bear Gulch

No. Fork Deer Creek

Curran G...

Deer Creek

Deer Creek Road

END

To Hwy 75

N

0 1 2 MILE

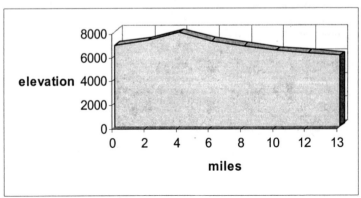

elevation

8000
6000
4000
2000
0

0 2 4 6 8 10 12 13

miles

30. The Bald Mountain Trails

The Sun Valley Company and the U.S. Forest Service have recently built a trail system on Bald Mountain Ski Area. You can either ride the lifts to the top of the mountain for a nominal charge or you can grind your way to the top. Either way is a spectacular experience. The trails are well marked with signs and maps the entire way. Please be considerate of other uphill riders and hikers during the descent.

Warm Springs Trail

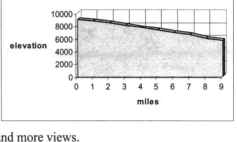

Length: 9.1 miles
Starting Elevation: 9010'
Ending Elevation: 5880'
Total Elevation Gain/Loss: 3130'
The Ride: One-way
Surface: Single track trail
Difficulty Rating: Difficult
Season: May - October
Fun Factor: Views, incredible views and more views.
Summary: If you're riding up the trail, it gradually climbs and switchbacks most of the way up this side of the mountain before gaining a ridge and winding its way to the top via the west side of the mountain. If you're riding down, be cautious of other riders and hikers moving in your opposite direction.
Trailhead Directions: From Ketchum Main Street, drive north turning left at the light leading to Warm Springs Road. Follow this road as it winds through a Ketchum business district and over the Big Wood River. Approximately 2 miles from Ketchum, at the four way stop sign, turn left leading to the base of Warm Springs side of Bald Mountain. The trailhead is located at the base of the ski run, next to the lodge.

Cold Springs Trail

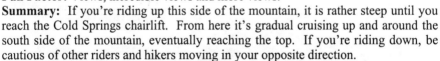

Length: 8.6 miles
Starting Elevation: 9010'
Ending Elevation: 5680'
Total Elevation Gain/Loss: 3330'
The Ride: One-way
Surface: Single track trail
Difficulty Rating: Difficult
Season: May - October
Fun Factor: Views, incredible views and more views.
Summary: If you're riding up this side of the mountain, it is rather steep until you reach the Cold Springs chairlift. From here it's gradual cruising up and around the south side of the mountain, eventually reaching the top. If you're riding down, be cautious of other riders and hikers moving in your opposite direction.
Trailhead Directions: From the Main Street (Hwy 75) and Sun Valley Road stop light in Ketchum, go west on Third Street heading toward the mountain. After four blocks the road takes a natural left and becomes Third Avenue. Follow this road as it winds its way to the River Run base of the mountain. Park here and backtrack on your bike about 100 feet to the bike path and ride south approximately 2 miles. Turn right at the trailhead sign and begin riding up Cold Springs canyon. If you passed under the highway on the bike path, you've gone about 100 yards too far.

Lower River Run Trail

Length: 9 miles
Starting Elevation: 5680'
High Point Elevation: 7350''
Total Elevation Gain: 1670'
The Ride: One-way
Surface: Single track trail
Difficulty Rating: Moderate/Difficult
Season: May - October

Fun Factor: Views, incredible views and more views.

Summary: This is a great post-work, quick ride that'll get you from one side of Bald Mountain to the other. It is also great access to the top of the mountain. There are maps the entire way, so you'll have to seriously try hard to get lost.

Trailhead Directions: From the Main Street (Hwy 75) and Sun Valley Road stop light in Ketchum, go west on Third Street heading toward the mountain. After four blocks the road takes a natural left and becomes Third Avenue. Follow this road as it winds its way to the River Run base of the mountain. Park anywhere near the ski lifts. Mount up and ride over the bridge between the two large buildings and veer right of the ski lift and look for the trailhead taking off left under the lift. It is 5 miles of casual climbing before the descent into Warm Springs. From there, take the roads back into town and back to the River Run side of Bald Mountain and your car.

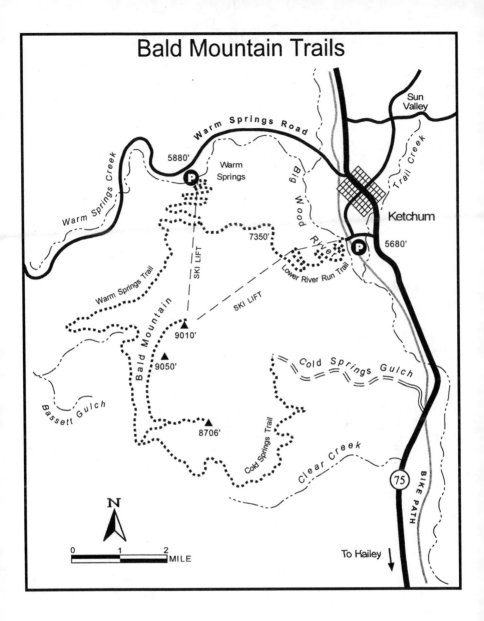

Bald Mountain Trails

Sun Valley

Warm Springs Road

Warm Springs Creek

5880'

Warm Springs

Big Wood River

Trail Creek

Ketchum

5680'

7350'

Lower River Run Trail

Warm Springs Trail

SKI LIFT

SKI LIFT

Bald Mountain

9010'

9050'

Cold Springs Gulch

Bassett Gulch

8706'

Cold Springs Trail

Clear Creek

75

BIKE PATH

N

0   1   2
MILE

To Hailey

31. Adams Gulch Area Rides

Adams Gulch is a heavily used area due to its close proximity to Ketchum. The trails here are used by hikers, trail runners, mountain bikers and equestrians. Please be considerate of others using the trails and stay in complete control while descending. The trails are not described in too much detail here, due to the signage throughout the area, as well as a very descriptive map at the parking area and in this guidebook. Ride mileages may vary depending where you start from. Some mileages are listed as "one-way" which doesn't mean it is rideable only in one direction, but rather the mileage is only from one end of the ride to the other.

Getting There: From Ketchum, drive north on Hwy 75 for 1.5 miles and turn left at the sign for Adams Gulch Road. Follow this road down and through the subdivision, crossing over the river and veering right. Approximately 1/4 mile later at the T-intersection, turn left and up the road, gaining the trailhead and parking area about 1 mile later.

Adams Gulch Loop

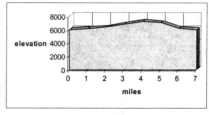

Length: 7 miles
Starting Elevation: 5950'
High Point Elevation: 7220'
Total Elevation Gain: 1270'
The Ride: loop
Surface: Dirt jeep road and single track trail
Difficulty Rating: Difficult
Season: Late May - October
Fun Factor: The ultimate loop complete with the complimentary grind.
Summary: Typically a clock-wise ride, you get a great warm-up on the jeep road before hitting the single track which is a constant grind to the top with periodic rests. Once topped out, the downhill is nothing short of spectacular. Well worth the work!

(This trail is sponsored by Backwoods Mtn Sports & Sun Summit Ski & Cycle)

Lane's / Sunnyside Trails

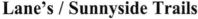

Length: 3.5 miles
Starting Elevation: 5950'
High Point Elevation: 6520'
Total Elevation Gain: 570'
The Ride: Loop
Surface: Dirt jeep road and single track trail
Difficulty Rating: Easy/Moderate
Season: May - October
Fun Factor: Picnic table rest at the top with phenomenal views.
Summary: While Shadyside is obviously in the shade, this one is directly opposite. You want sun? Come and get it! We like riding this one clock-wise, due to the gradual warm-up on the jeep road. Once it hits the single track, you grind for a bit before backing off and topping out at a picnic table. From here the descent is fun, fast and furious.

(This trail is sponsored by The Elephants Perch)

Shadyside Trail

Length: 3 miles
Starting Elevation: 5950'
High Point Elevation: 6200'
Total Elevation Gain: 250'
The Ride: Loop
Surface: Dirt jeep road and single track trail
Difficulty Rating: Easy/Moderate
Season: Late May - October

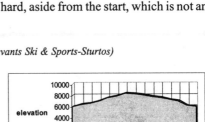

Fun Factor: A definite fun warm up on a hot summer day.
Summary: This ride is never too technical or hard, aside from the start, which is not an indicator for the rest of the ride.

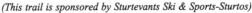

(This trail is sponsored by Sturtevants Ski & Sports-Sturtos)

Adams Gulch Trail

Length: 14 miles
Starting Elevation: 5950'
High Point Elevation: 8400'
Total Elevation Gain: 2450'
The Ride: Loop
Surface: Dirt jeep road and single track trail
Difficulty Rating: Abusive
Season: Late May - October

Fun Factor: This ride defines the word fun. Hills, views and downhills.
Summary: This is a serious ride. It seems longer than it is due to its technical nature. Have the right attitude from the onset or don't go.

Harpers Trail

Length: 3.5 miles
Starting Elevation: 5950'
High Point Elevation: 7000'
Total Elevation Gain: 1050'
The Ride: Loop
Surface: Single track trail
Difficulty Rating: Moderate/Difficult
Season: Late May - October

Fun Factor: Another great loop which connects Fox Creek and Lake Creek into the Adams Gulch Area.
Summary: Great in either direction, but we personally like this one counter-clockwise. A short grind leads to rollers into Lake Creek area before gradual grinding up to the top where you encounter the Adams Gulch Loop descent.

(This trail is sponsored by the SVSEF with Fox Creek Linkage sponsored by Chateau Drug)

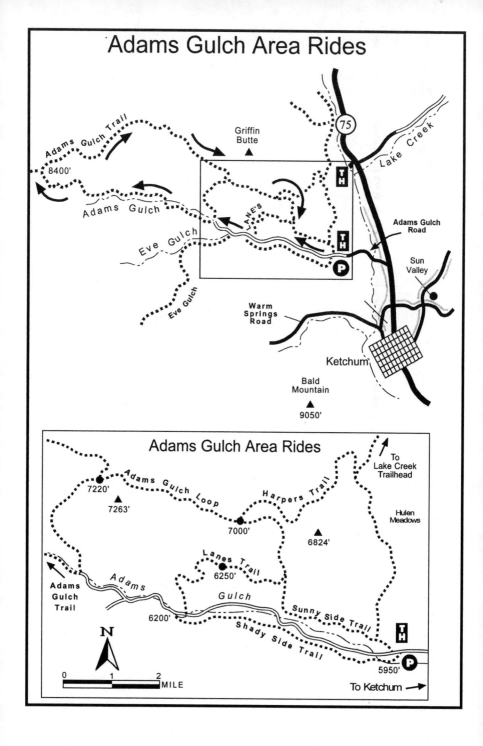

Adams Gulch Area Rides

Griffin Butte ▲

75

Lake Creek

Adams Gulch Trail

8400'

Adams Gulch

Eve Gulch

LANE'S

TH

TH

P

Adams Gulch Road

Sun Valley

Eve Gulch

Warm Springs Road

Ketchum

Bald Mountain ▲ 9050'

Adams Gulch Area Rides

Adams Gulch Loop

7220'

▲ 7263'

Harpers Trail

7000'

To Lake Creek Trailhead

Hulen Meadows

▲ 6824'

Lanes Trail

6250'

Adams

Adams Gulch Trail

Gulch

6200'

Sunny Side Trail

Shady Side Trail

TH

P

5950'

N

0   1   2
MILE

To Ketchum →

32. Lake Creek

Length: 10 miles
Starting Elevation: 6100'
High Point Elevation: 6800'
Total Elevation Gain: 700'
The Ride: Out & back
Surface: Dirt jeep road
Difficulty Rating: Easy
Season: Mid-April through late-October
Fun Factor: Fishing, wildlife and a box canyon.
Summary: If you're in need of a casual and fun ride to introduce yourselves to Wood River mountain biking, this is a good start. Pack your fishing rod and add to the experience by enjoying the stocked lake for fishing and picnicing.
Getting There: From Ketchum, drive north on Highway 75 for 3.1 miles and turn right onto Lake Creek Road. Drive up the main road for approximately 1 mile to where you reach a cul-de-sac. Park here and please respect the private property. The ride begins here.

Miles	The Ride:
0.0	Begin by riding up the dirt road paralleling the fence on the northeast side of the cul-de-sac.
3.5	After rolling along the road for what seems to be quite a ways, look for wildlife. Soon, you will encounter the Lake Creek lakes. Unpack your picnic and hang out here for a bit, or head up the road for better views and cruising.
5.0	End of the trail. The road forks here with the left trail eventually touching down in Eagle Creek drainage while the right fork heads up Trail Creek via Rock Roll Canyon. Both forks are steep, strenuous and for the adventure-minded only. (Summer 2000 the authors could not find these trails.)
10.0	The end of the ride and back at your car.

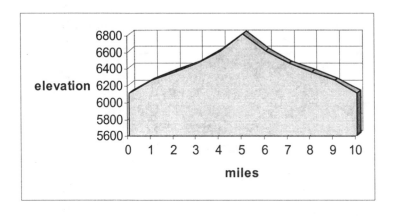

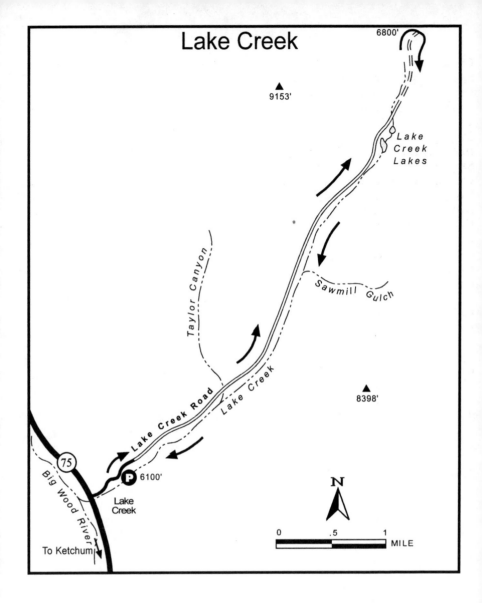

Lake Creek

6800'

9153'

Lake
Creek
Lakes

Taylor Canyon

Sawmill Gulch

8398'

Lake Creek Road

Lake Creek

75

Big Wood River

P 6100'

Lake
Creek

To Ketchum

N

0 .5 1 MILE

33. Fox Creek

Length: 6.6 miles
Starting Elevation: 5950'
High Point Elevation: 6700'
Total Elevation Gain: 750'
The Ride: Loop
Surface: Single track trail and dirt jeep road.
Difficulty Rating: Moderate/Difficult
Season: Late May - October
Fun Factor: Moderate climbs, great descents, and wildflowers.
Summary: This is undoubtedly one of the best all-around rides close to Ketchum. Never too steep to ride and always a good time on the downhills.
Getting There: From Ketchum, drive north on Highway 75 for 4 miles to the Lake Creek Trailhead and turn left into the parking lot. The ride begins here. (**Access to the Lake Creek Trailhead may be hindered by flood waters in early season. If this is the case, turn around and drive back 0.5 miles on the highway to Hulen Meadows Road and turn right. Follow the road across the bridge, and park on the right immediately in the gravel parking area. Ride up the road staying right until the cul-de-sac. Follow the trail next to the driveway heading north at the end of the cul-de-sac. In 1/4 mile you join up with the main Lake Creek trail coming in from the right.

Miles	The Ride:
0.0	From the Lake Creek trailhead parking lot, ride across the steel bridge and the Big Wood River. Follow this trail as it winds to the right through the trees and next to the river.
0.2	Ride up a small embankment to where it intersects with a jeep road. Turn right here.
0.6	Trail junction: The left fork here is where the Fox Creek Loop comes out. Stay straight on the jeep trail heading north.
1.3	The jeep road turns to single track and quickly comes to a shale/rock traverse. After roller-coastering along, you will cross two small bridges.
1.9	An intensely steep switchback leads up and away from the river, followed by a similarly steep downhill and a quick slalom course through the aspen trees.
2.4	Cross over Fox Creek and come to a trail junction: Turn left here on the Fox Creek Trail. The right fork will put you on the North Fork Trail.
2.6	Another trail junction: Take the left (straight) fork to continue heading up stream into Fox Creek. The right fork leads into the upper section of the North Fork Loop.
3.1	After crossing over two bridges, you reach another trail junction. Stay on the left (straight) fork heading upstream into Fox Creek. The right fork leads to Oregon Gulch and/or Chocolate Gulch. From here the trail becomes a "one-way" only trail for mountain bikers. Be cautious here, runners and hikers could be coming in the other direction. After a couple 100 yards cross over Fox Creek and begin a gradual climb up switchbacks.

4.1 Come to a saddle and continue on. The faint trail off to the right of the trail here leads to a nice bench in the meadow.

6.0 Join the main trail again as the loop is now complete. Turn right and continue back to the trail head at Lake Creek or Hulen Meadows.

6.6 End of the ride and back at your car.

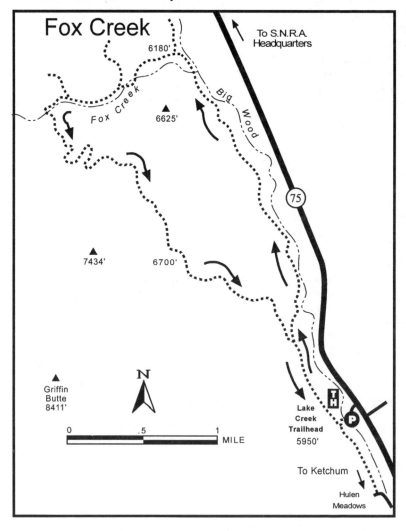

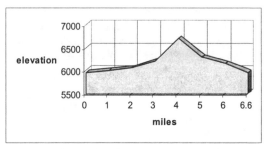

34. Eagle Creek

Length: 8.8 miles
Starting Elevation: 6250'
High Point Elevation: 7100'
Total Elevation Gain: 850'
The Ride: Out & back
Surface: Dirt jeep road
Difficulty Rating: Moderate
Season: Early-May - late October
Fun Factor: Beautiful valley, wildlife and high peaks.
Summary: This is such a great evening ride for any level of mountain biker. Following the creek is incredible with great chances of seeing elk, deer, wolf and bear.
Getting There: From Ketchum, drive north on Highway 75 approximately 6.3 miles to Eagle Creek Road and turn right here. Follow the pavement up past the "dead end" sign and veer right past the driveway and onto the dirt jeep road in the trees. Park here.

<u>Miles</u>	<u>The Ride:</u>
0.0	Begin by riding northeast on the dirt road heading up the valley and away from the homes.
0.2	Enter the Sawtooth National Forest. You'll notice you're on Rd #144.
0.6	Road on the right reads "Neals Canyon," which goes approx. 100 yds before ending at a primitive campsite. The trail up the canyon is a steep hiking trail.
1.5	Creek crossing to a small climb into a nice alpine meadow.
1.9	Road on the right leads nowhere. Stay on the main road as it closes in.
3.6	After crossing the creek 3 times by now, you can see the end of the canyon.
4.4	Top of the ride. There is usually tons of avalanche debris around this area. If you're feeling a bit adventurous, try to find the faint jeep trail leading up and south into Lake Creek. The word "adventurous" is the key here. (Summer 2000 the authors couldn't find the trail to Lake Creek).
8.8	The end of the ride and back at your car.

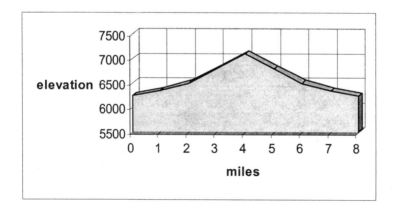

Eagle Creek

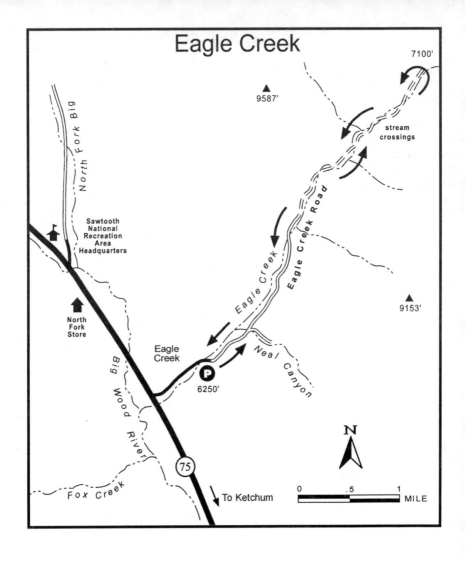

35. Chocolate Gulch

Length: 3.8 miles
Starting Elevation: 6150'
High Point Elevation: 6750'
Total Elevation Gain: 600'
The Ride: Loop
Surface: Single track trail
Difficulty Rating: Moderate/Difficult
Season: Mid-May - late October
Fun Factor: Moderate climbing to incredible views of the Wood River Valley.
Summary: This is a rather short but fun ride that has moderate climbing, creek cross-ings, technical rock moves, views and a great descent. On top of that, it has access to three other rides in the immediate surrounding area.
Getting There: From Ketchum, drive north on Highway 75 approximately 6.8 miles and turn left on Chocolate Gulch Road (just after crossing over the Big Wood River). Drive to the end of the road and park here. This parking area can usually get crowded so please respect the private property and only park in the designated area. If it is too crowded in the parking area please choose another ride or park at the Oregon Gulch parking area just north about 1/2 mile.

<u>Miles</u>	<u>The Ride:</u>
0.0	From the parking area ride west and immediately onto the single track which takes a quick switchback to the left and gradually climbs a bit to the Choco-late Gulch trail #149B. Turn right here.
0.3	After crossing a small bridge, a muddy bog and the stream, take a sharp left around the willows and start a gradual climb, passing by the right fork for Saddle Trail which leads over the hills to Oregon Gulch (1.9 mi. long).
0.6	Forge another stream crossing leading to moderate climbing.
1.5	Top of the first saddle. This is a false summit, keep going, almost there!
1.7	Top of the second saddle and the high-point of the ride. Continue on down the trail passing by a difficult rock/sand/scree pile and into a couple of switchbacks. Be careful here, the trail could be fairly loose.
2.1	Junction. The left fork is the continuation of the Chocolate Gulch trail, while the right fork is the Oregon Gulch/Fox Creek Loop #149C. Make a left turn here.
2.4	Junction. The left fork is the continuation of the Chocolate Gulch trail along with Fox Creek Loop (you are now on one trail of two different names). Don't get confused, just look at the sign. Go left here. Taking the right trail would lead to the upper section of Fox Creek.
2.7	After a few roller-coasters, you cross over Fox Creek on two bridges.
2.9	Junction. Take the left fork here on the North Fork Loop #149A and start climbing up a switchback. It seems steep but is relatively short.
3.5	Junction with the lower section of the North Fork Loop. Continue straight.
3.8	End of the ride and back at the trailhead.

(This trail is sponsored by Premier Resorts)

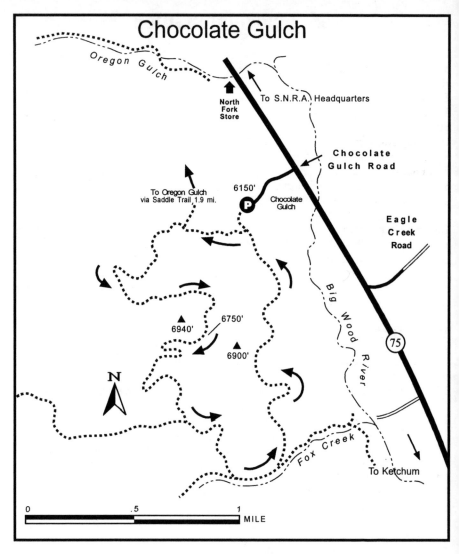

Chocolate Gulch

Oregon Gulch

North Fork Store

To S.N.R.A. Headquarters

Chocolate Gulch Road

6150'

To Oregon Gulch via Saddle Trail 1.9 mi.

Chocolate Gulch

Eagle Creek Road

▲ 6940'

6750'

▲ 6900'

Big Wood River

75

N

Fox Creek

To Ketchum

0   .5   1

MILE

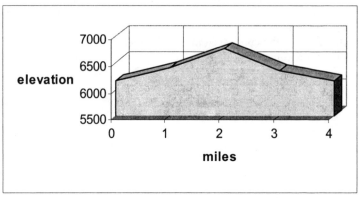

elevation

7000
6500
6000
5500

0   1   2   3   4

miles

36. North Fork Loop

Length: 2.6 miles
Starting Elevation: 6150'
High Point Elevation: 6350'
Total Elevation Gain: 200'
The Ride: Loop
Surface: Single track trail
Difficulty Rating: Moderate/Difficult
Season: Early May - late October
Fun Factor: Quick, technical, views and river.
Summary: The North Fork Loop is usually considered as a starting point for other rides. However, the loop in itself is a great warm-up for Chocolate Gulch or Fox Creek.
Getting There: From Ketchum, drive north on Highway 75 approximately 6.8 miles and turn left on Chocolate Gulch Road (just after crossing over the Big Wood River). Drive to the end of the road and park here. This parking area can usually get a bit crowded so please respect the private property and only park in the designated area. If it is too crowded in the parking area please choose another ride or park in the Oregon Gulch parking area about half mile north on the highway.

Miles	The Ride:
0.0	From the parking area ride west and immediately onto the single track which takes a quick switchback to the left and gradually climbs a bit passing the Chocolate Gulch trail #149B on the right. Stay straight on the main trail here.
0.3	Junction with the North Fork Loop trail #149A. Go right here. From here be careful as the trail crosses over a steep hillside and rocks.
0.4	Gain a small saddle then immediately drop into a creek and immediately climb a short hill.
1.0	After the trail roller-coasters a bit, you gain another saddle and begin the descent into Fox Creek.
1.3	Junction with Fox Creek. The North Fork Loop goes to the left here. If you want to combine any other ride in the area, going right would lead to Chocolate Gulch, Fox Creek or Oregon Gulch.
1.5	Junction. The left fork leads on into the rest of the North Fork Loop. The right fork leads to the Lake Creek trailhead and Fox Creek.
2.1	Skinny bridge, be careful here especially when it is wet.
2.3	A steep pitch leads back to the beginning of the loop. Turn right at the top, continuing on the same trail.
2.6	After passing back by the Chocolate Gulch trailhead you find yourself back at the car and the end of the ride.

(This trail is sponsored by the authors of Good Dirt II and Ultimate Direction hydration packs)

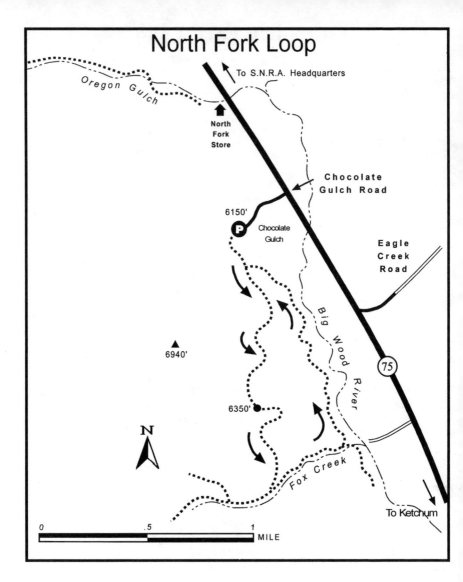

North Fork Loop

To S.N.R.A. Headquarters

Oregon Gulch

North Fork Store

Chocolate Gulch Road

6150'

Chocolate Gulch

Eagle Creek Road

Big Wood River

6940'

6350'

75

N

Fox Creek

To Ketchum

0 .5 1 MILE

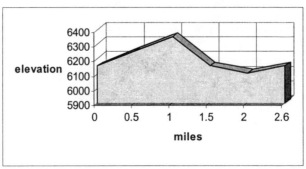

elevation

6400
6300
6200
6100
6000
5900

0   0.5   1   1.5   2   2.6

miles

37. Oregon Gulch

Length: 11.0 miles
Starting Elevation: 6250'
High Point Elevation: 7600'
Total Elevation Gain: 2310'
The Ride: Loop
Surface: Single track trail
Difficulty Rating: Difficult
Season: June through October
Fun Factor: Climbs, long downhills, streams, wildflowers.
Summary: This is one of those rides that is such a great time, you forget about the technical part instantly. Rock outcrops will test your balance and downhills will test your nerves.
Getting There: From Ketchum, drive north on Highway 75 for just over 7 miles to the North Fork Store. Turn left on the dirt road just past the store and behind the trailers. Follow this back to a grassy meadow with bathrooms. Park here.

Miles	The Ride:
0.0	Begin by riding up the single track trail on the west side of the parking area.
0.2	After entering into the trees you will encounter a junction with a trail leading over Saddle Trail (1.9 miles long) on the left and eventually into Chocolate Gulch. Instead, stay straight on the main trail which quickly goes down and over the creek where the trail continues up the gulch on the north side of the creek. This is Oregon Gulch.
1.3	Cross through the gate (please close it behind you).
3.2	Trail junction: Turn left here and cross the creek heading toward Fox Creek. The right fork goes up and eventually into the East Fork of Baker Creek.
4.6	Saddle, watch for the sharp right turn in about 100 yards.
5.0	Climb to a saddle and turn left into the gulch. The more worn right fork just climbs to a small overlook. From here the trail becomes a technical steep downhill with loose dirt and rocks.
7.0	Trail junction: Turn right and continue on the Oregon/Fox Creek Loop #149C. The left fork climbs up and over into Chocolate Gulch on Trail #146B.
7.25	Trail junction: Turn left and head downstream with Fox Creek.
7.5	After a few roller-coasters, you cross over Fox Creek on two bridges.
7.7	Junction. Take the left fork here on the North Fork Loop #149A and start climbing up a switch-back to a saddle.
8.3	Pass by the junction with the lower section of the North Fork Loop.
8.6	Turn left at the sign leading to Chocolate Gulch.
8.9	Turn right at the sign leading to Saddle Trail.
10.8	Back at the junction with Oregon Gulch Trail. Turn right here.
11.0	End of the ride and back at your car.

(This trail sponsored by Biy Wood Backcountry Trails, Ketchum/SV Rotary, Williams Market & Adventure Press)

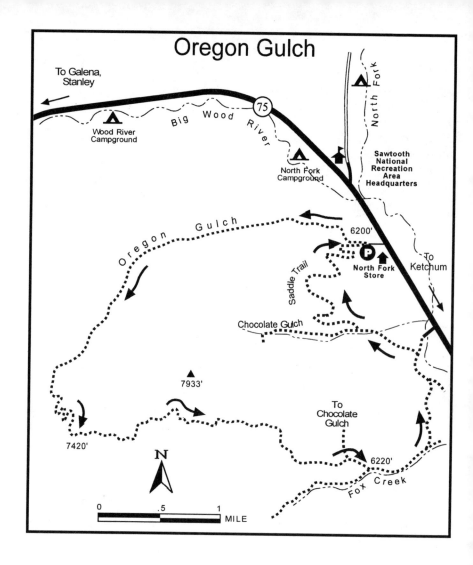

Oregon Gulch

To Galena, Stanley

Wood River Campground

Big Wood River

75

North Fork Campground

North Fork

Sawtooth National Recreation Area Headquarters

Oregon Gulch

6200'

Saddle Trail

North Fork Store

To Ketchum

Chocolate Gulch

7933'

7420'

N

To Chocolate Gulch

6220'

Fox Creek

0   .5   1
MILE

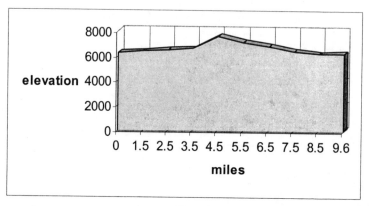

38. North Fork Big Wood River

Length: 10.2 miles
Starting Elevation: 6240'
High Point Elevation: 6900'
Total Elevation Gain: 660'
The Ride: Out and back
Surface: Dirt jeep road
Difficulty Rating: Easy
Season: Late April - late October
Fun Factor: Endless picnic spots, big valley views and the North Fork of Big Wood River.
Summary: Let's say you need a ride you can take wine, cheese and crackers on. Let's say you need to take some charcoal too. This is your ride, complete with permanent BBQs already in position just waiting for you at any number of the camp and picnic sites.
Getting There: From Ketchum, drive 7.8 miles north on Highway 75 to the turn off for the Sawtooth National Recreation Area headquarters (SNRA). Turn right here and park in the main parking lot.

Miles	The Ride:
0.0	Begin by riding out of the parking lot and north on the main paved road where it quickly turns to dirt and gravel.
1.1	Cross over the North Fork of the Big Wood River. Just after the bridge, the road forks. The right fork goes up Murdock Creek (worth exploring if you have the time), but stay on the main road heading north up the main drainage.
3.5	After crossing the junction of the East Fork and North Forks of the Big Wood River, Camp Manapu is off to the right.
3.7	Road to the right leads to the East Fork of the Big Wood River and a pretty interesting single track hiking trail.
5.1	Top of the ride at the North Fork Trailhead. The trails that continue up the two canyons from here become difficult to negotiate but offer some great hiking opportunities. Turn around here and head back down.
10.2	End of the ride and back at your car.

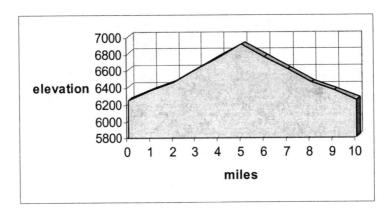

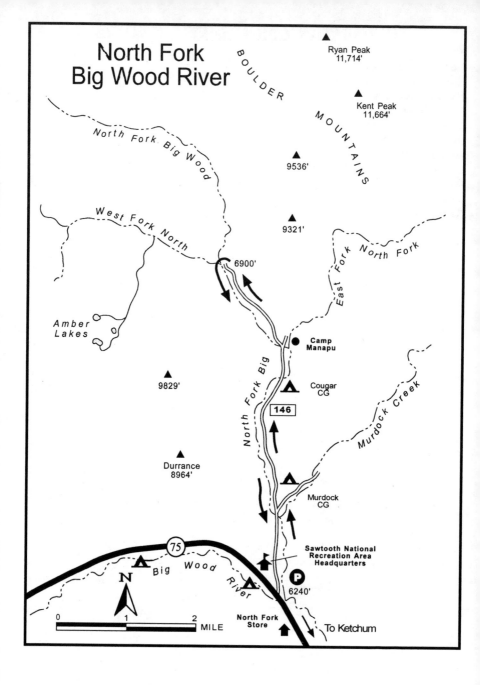

North Fork
Big Wood River

BOULDER MOUNTAINS

Ryan Peak
11,714'

Kent Peak
11,664'

9536'

North Fork Big Wood

West Fork North

9321'

East Fork North Fork

6900'

Amber
Lakes

Camp
Manapu

Cougar
CG

146

Murdock Creek

9829'

North Fork Big

Durrance
8964'

Murdock
CG

Sawtooth National
Recreation Area
Headquarters

75

P
6240'

N

Big Wood River

0   1   2
|___|___|___| MILE

North Fork
Store

To Ketchum

39. Fox Peak

Length: 22.4 miles
Starting Elevation: 6675'
High Point Elevation: 8720'
Total Elevation Gain: 2045'
The Ride: One-way
Surface: Dirt jeep road to single track trail
Difficulty Rating: Abusive
Season: June - October
Fun Factor: Wicked downhills, climbs and traverses.
Summary: This is not a first date ride. Be ready for going over the front of your bike, falling and pushing.
Getting There: From Ketchum, drive north on Highway 75 approximately 15.5 miles and park on the right side of the road directly opposite of Baker Creek Road. The ride begins here.

<u>Miles</u>	<u>The Ride:</u>
0.0	From the parking area, cross back over the highway and begin riding up Baker Creek Road #162.
3.1	Just after crossing over the East Fork of Baker Creek, turn left onto the East Fork of Baker Creek Road #68 and begin a gradual climb.
5.1	At the fork, take the lower (left), more traveled road which descends for a bit before climbing again.
5.7	When you come to the next fork, take the right (upper), more traveled road and begin climbing another pitch.
6.3	Encounter the switchbacks which are never too hard.
8.0	The saddle with a view. Continue on the jeep road passing by the trailhead to the Easley Loop around the next corner.
9.6	Pass by the Oregon Gulch access trailhead on the left.
9.7	Begin a fast descent on the jeep road, but keep a watch for a single-track turn-off in another 1.6 miles. It's easy to miss, unless you mean to.
11.3	Sign on the left says trail for Fox Creek and Adams Gulch. You can go this way if you want, but you'll have to push a bit. Instead, stay on the main road.
12.3	At the major intersection, stay left!
12.6	The double track dead ends at a berm. Single-track starts on the back side.
13.0	Trail junction: Stay left on Trail #142 to Adams Gulch.
14.0	Gain a small grassy saddle and begin a quick, exciting downhill.
14.2	Trail junction: The right fork leads into the top of Adams Gulch. Instead, stay straight on the main trail traversing the hillside. From here to the junction with Adams Gulch Loop, the trail is rocky, loose and intense in some places.
17.8	After climbing a short steep hill, the trail traverses down and into Adams Gulch.
19.3	Trail junction: You are now at the top of the Adams Gulch Loop Trail. Either direction (L or R) will take you down to the trailhead. But why not keep the fun rolling? Turn left.

20.2   Harpers Trail takes off to the left, but stay straight on Adams Gulch Loop.
22.4   The end of the ride and the parking area.

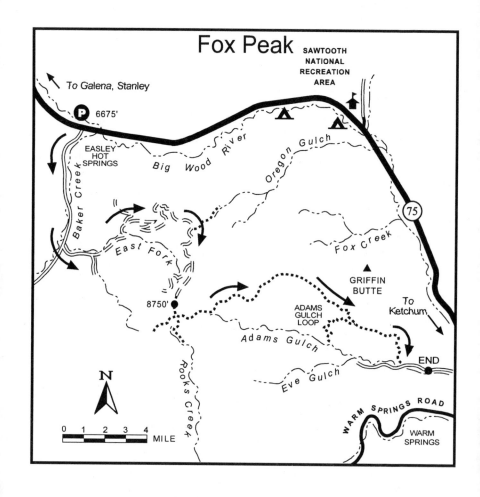

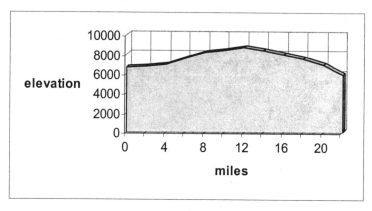

Stanley Lake in the Sawtooth Mountains, circa 1930
Courtesy of Community Library, Ketchum, Idaho, Regional History Department

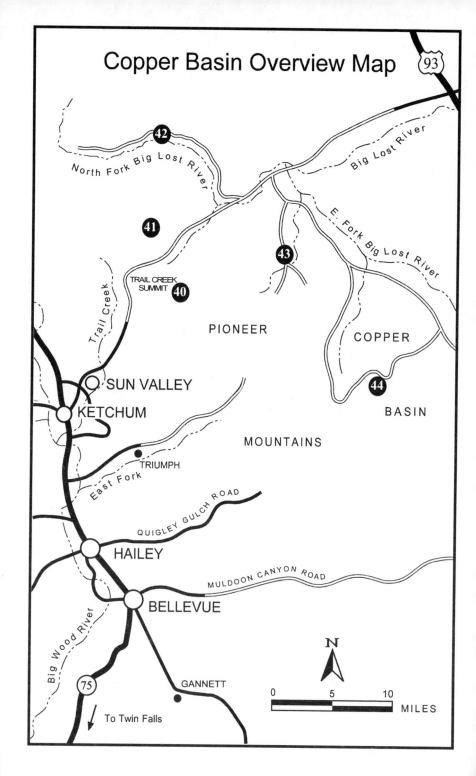

Copper Basin Overview Map

40. Summit Creek

Length: 19.5 miles
Starting Elevation: 7894'
High Point Elevation: 9480'
Total Elevation Gain: 1586' (2360' for entire loop)
The Ride: Loop
Surface: Single track trail, dirt jeep road and gravel road
Difficulty Rating: Difficult/Abusive
Season: June - September
Fun Factor: Incredible views of the Pioneer Mountains, wildlife and wild flowers.
Summary: With stunning views the entire time, you are given the climax right at the top of this pump-fest, oxygen-deprived ride with the Devils Bedstead.
Getting There: From the Main Street/Sun Valley Road interection in Ketchum, drive east toward Sun Valley Resort. Continue on up the road eventually turning into Trail Creek Road. After 12.5 miles you reach Trail Creek Summit. Park in the area on the right just over the summit and begin the ride here. If you are shuttling a car to do the one-way version of this ride, continue driving down the road approximately 7.5 miles until the Kane Creek Road. Park on the right.

Miles	The Ride:
0.0	From the parking area, ride up through the parking area until the obvious trail is in front of you. Cross that creek and begin climbing up a rather steep but rideable switchback.
0.75	After the trail levels out a bit, you cruise through a sometimes wet meadow then cross Summit Creek again. From here the trail is a fun series of gradual climbs and beautiful meadows for about 3 miles.
3.0	The trail begins its famous 1 mile climbing section with steep pitches then semi-level breathers afterward. Hang in there, the view is well worth it!
4.0	The top of Summit Creek! Looking to the east, you'll see the Devils Bedstead looming over your head (11,051 ft). Now start by looking for the trail heading down into Kane Creek off the top of the summit (left). The trail is not obvious,but if you continue down to your left into Kane Creek, you will find it. If you ride forward on the trail instead of left off the top you'll ride into a boulder field. Look for cairns and other obvious trail signs.
6.8	Junction with the Kane Creek trail. Go left and down to the parking area.
7.2	Kane Creek parking lot, ride down the obvious road toward Trail Creek Road. An option is to turn left in ~3.5 miles and take the shorter alternative route.
12.1	Junction with Trail Creek Road. If you parked here, crack a liquid refreshment and drive on back to Ketchum. If you only own 1 car like most of us and left it at the summit of Trail Creek Road, saddle up, take a left turn and huff it the 7.5 miles and 775 ft back up to your car.
19.5	The end of the ride.

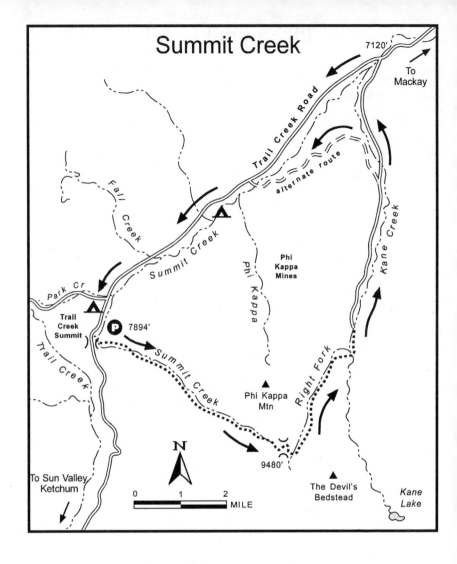

Summit Creek

7120'

To Mackay

Trail Creek Road

alternate route

Fall Creek

Summit Creek

Phi Kappa Mines

Kane Creek

Park Cr

Trail Creek Summit

P 7894'

Summit Creek

Phi Kappa

Right Fork

Trail Creek

Phi Kappa Mtn

N

To Sun Valley Ketchum

0   1   2 MILE

9480'

The Devil's Bedstead

Kane Lake

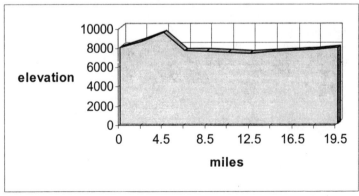

elevation

10000
8000
6000
4000
2000
0

0   4.5   8.5   12.5   16.5   19.5

miles

41. Park Creek

Length: 12.4 miles
Starting Elevation: 7646'
High Point Elevation: 8500'
Total Elevation Gain: 854'
The Ride: Out and back
Surface: Dirt jeep road and single track trail
Difficulty Rating: Moderate
Season: Late May - October
Fun Factor: Gorgeous canyon, wildlife and trail finding.
Summary: Parker Creek is one of those hidden wonders in the Copper Basin area, where beautiful canyons, creeks, fishing and camping make for an entire weekend experience. The trail is a bit rough in places.
Getting There: From the Main Street/Sun Valley Road interection in Ketchum, drive east toward Sun Valley, passing the resort complex area and continue on up the road eventually becoming Trail Creek Road. After 12.5 miles you reach Trail Creek Summit. Continue on the main road for another 0.7 miles and park on the left at the junction of Park Creek Road #140 and Trail Creek. The ride begins here.

<u>Miles</u>	<u>The Ride:</u>
0.0	Begin by riding up road #140 heading north and west through a large meadow.
1.2	Road to the left leads to the High Ridge Trail trailhead. Continue on Parker Creek Road up the canyon. For the next 1.5 miles you'll encounter many primitive campsites and meadows.
2.7	Major stream crossing over Parker Creek.
3.9	Whoa! Look for the cairn on the right of the road to show you where to cross the creek (A little ways further the main road fades away into nothing). Instead, cross the creek, look for a faint trail leading uphill and into some trees. There you'll find a better trail leading left (north). This is not too difficult to find. Sounds difficult, but it snot.
4.3	A stream crossing leads to a series of springs and mud bogs.
4.7	Encounter another small meadow with bogs.
4.9	Whoa! After a steep crossing over a small creek, veer left on the other side of the creek following the contour of the creek and looking for the cairns.
5.0	Be sure to follow the trail heading left at all of the downed timber. From here the trail begins climbing up the canyon following the creek at all times.
5.4	The trail contours the creek at a very steep angle here.
6.2	At the edge of the completely downed forest in front of you is the end of the ride. After exploring further up the canyon from here, I'm convinced that a chainsaw is mandatory equipment, I just haven't found the proper bike mount...yet. Turn around and retrace your route. This ride could be an even better loop if someone had the will and power to do some logging.
12.4	The end of the ride and back at your car.

Park Creek

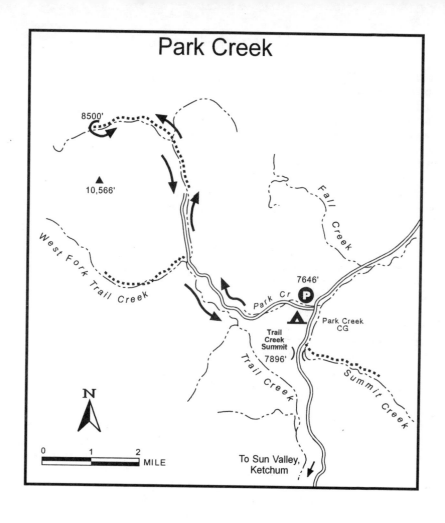

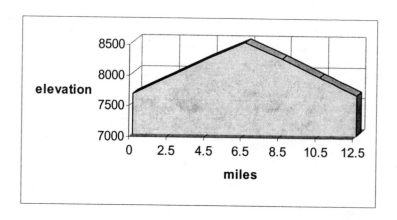

42. North Fork Big Lost River

Length: 26.4 miles
Starting Elevation: 7100'
High Point Elevation: 8120'
Total Elevation Gain: 1020'
The Ride: Out and back
Surface: Dirt jeep road
Difficulty Rating: Easy
Season: May - October
Fun Factor: Incredible views of the Pioneer and Boulder Mountains.
Summary: When you feel like getting away from the commotion of the Wood River Valley and need to escape for a day or a weekend, this is the ride for solitude. Breathtaking views of the Devils Bedstead and the Boulder Mountains make it even better.
Getting There: From the stop light in Ketchum, at the Main Street and Sun Valley Road intersection, drive east up Sun Valley Road heading toward Trail Creek. After reaching the summit at 12.5 miles, continue 7.8 miles to North Fork Big Lost River Road on the left. Turn left here and park by the river. The ride begins here.

<u>Miles</u>	<u>The Ride:</u>
0.0	Begin by riding up the North Fork Big Lost River Road.
1.1	Round the corner in the main drainage with a few homesteads on the left side. Be sure and look over your shoulder at this point to see an incredible view of the Devils Bedstead. Continue up the main road.
3.9	A pack trail takes off to the right up Horse Creek. Do not go that way.
6.0	Phenomenal views of the Boulder Mountains. Ryan and Kent peaks are in front of you.
6.5	Toolbox Creek takes off to the right. Do not go that way either.
7.1	At the top of the climb a spur road takes off to the right. Stay on the main road and descend to the valley floor.
7.4	Park Canyon Road spurs off to the right, stay on the main road.
9.0	Miller Canyon Road goes to the left. Stay on the main road. The views just keep getting better the further you go up the North Fork drainage.
11.4	Hunter Creek Trail spurs off to the right. Stay on the main road. Hunter Creek offers an overland route to Bowery Hot Springs area on the East Fork of the Salmon River.
11.7	Start climbing up an old logging road passing a junction at 12.1 miles and eventually reaching the end of the road.
13.2	The top of the ride. This is also the start of the trailhead to North Fork Lake which exits the parking area on the west though some clear cuts and eventually to the base of Ryan Peak. Not advised for mountain bikes, but is a great hike for another day.
26.4	The end of the ride and back at your car.

North Fork Big Lost River

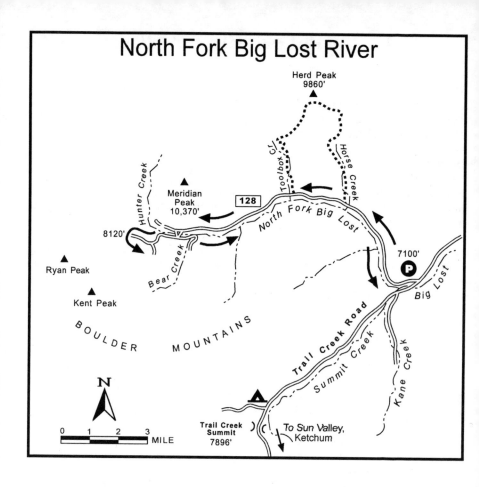

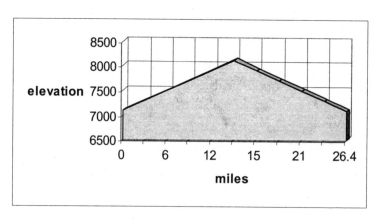

43. Wildhorse Creek

Length: 12.2 miles
Starting Elevation: 7180'
High Point Elevation: 7320'
Total Elevation Gain: 140'
The Ride: Out and back
Surface: Dirt and gravel jeep roads
Difficulty Rating: Easy
Season: May - October
Fun Factor: The Pioneer Mountains, antelope and great fishing!
Summary: Some people think of the Copper Basin area as rather desolate and dusty. Well, it is. However, just off the beaten paths you find little gold mines and beautiful rides. This is just one of them.
Getting There: From the main stop light in Ketchum, at the intersection of Main Street and Sun Valley Road, drive east up Sun Valley Road heading toward Trail Creek. After reaching the summit at 12.5 miles, drive 10.3 miles to Wildhorse/Copper Basin Road #135. Turn right and drive down the road 2 miles to the junction of Copper Basin Road and Wildhorse Creek Road. Park here.

Miles	The Ride:
0.0	Begin riding up the road toward Wildhorse Creek with incredible views of the Pioneer Mountains.
1.0	Pass the Wildhorse Guard Station on the left.
2.1	Burnt Aspen and Kane Creek trailhead on the right. Stay on the main road.
3.5	At the junction, stay on the main road. The left fork leads to Falls Creek.
4.1	Just another shabby view of the Pioneers.
5.6	Boulder Creek trailhead on the right. Stay on the main road past here.
5.8	The Wildhorse Campground.
6.1	Top of the ride at the end of the campground. There is a trailhead here marked by a "rough narrow road" sign. If you are interested in more strenuous biking from here, follow the road for approximately 3.5 miles to the Wildhorse Mines. This is a fun ride, but be sure to stock up on your bug spray, the horse flys can be vicious in the late part of the summer.
12.2	The end of the ride and back at your car.

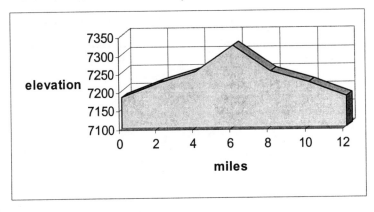

Wildhorse Creek

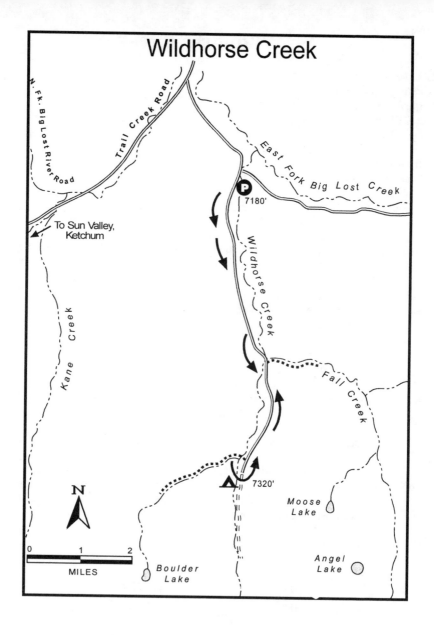

N. Fk. Big Lost River Road

Trail Creek Road

East Fork Big Lost Creek

P 7180'

To Sun Valley, Ketchum

Wildhorse Creek

Kane Creek

Fall Creek

N

7320'

Moose Lake

0   1   2
MILES

Boulder Lake

Angel Lake

44. Lake Creek (Copper Basin)

Length: 13.8 miles
Starting Elevation: 8080'
High Point Elevation: 9650'
Total Elevation Gain: 1570'
The Ride: Out and back
Surface: Single track trail
Difficulty Rating: Difficult
Season: June - October
Fun Factor: The Pioneer Mountains, lakes and great fishing!
Summary: Truly one of the classics of Copper Basin. Put your fun-hat on and get ready for a great ride amidst lakes and the Pioneer Mountains.
Getting There: From the stop light in Ketchum, at the Main Street and Sun Valley Road intersection, drive east up Sun Valley Road heading toward Trail Creek Summit. After reaching the summit at 12.5 miles, drive 10.3 miles to Wildhorse/Copper Basin Road #135. Turn right and drive down the road 2 miles to the junction of Copper Basin Road and Wildhorse Creek Road. Turn left here and drive another 16 dusty miles (it's worth it), turning right at the second Copper Basin Loop Road sign. Cruise another 4.5 miles up the road to the Lake Creek turn-off. Park here, this is where the ride begins.

Miles	The Ride:
0.0	Begin by riding up the trail, slowly winding your way up the valley, eventually getting to a rather large meadow.
3.9	At the fork near the cabin, turn left and get ready for a bit of a grind.
6.1	Catch your breath and pass by the trail over to Round Lake, the first of four lakes.
6.6	Cruise past Long Lake, or stop to cool off.
7.5	After a short steep pitch, you arrive at Rough Lake.
8.6	The final of four lakes, Big Lake, is reached after a short, gradual ascent.
9.8	Back at the original start of the lollipop loop. Turn left and continue back to the trailhead.
13.8	End of the ride and back at your car.

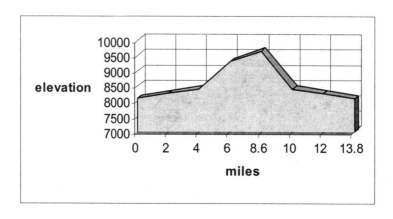

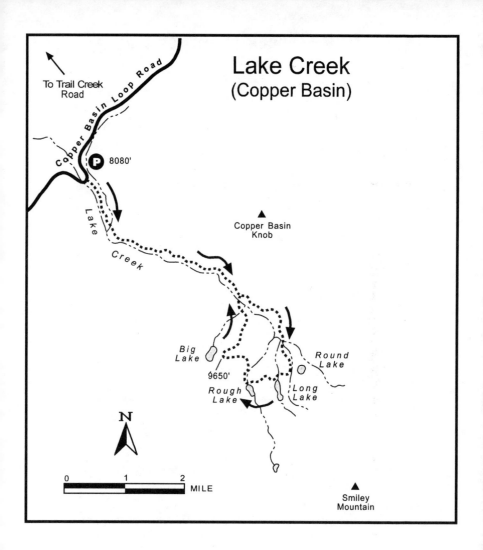

Lake Creek
(Copper Basin)

To Trail Creek Road

Copper Basin Loop Road

P 8080'

Lake Creek

Copper Basin Knob

Big Lake

9650'

Round Lake

Rough Lake

Long Lake

N

0   1   2 MILE

Smiley Mountain

Crossing over Galena Summit on the old Wagon Road, circa 1914
Courtesy of Community Library, Ketchum, Idaho, Regional History Department

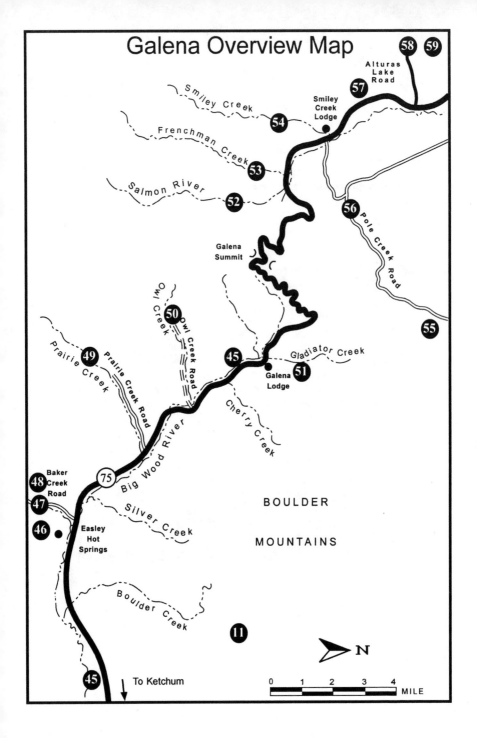

Galena Overview Map

Alturas Lake Road

Smiley Creek

Smiley Creek Lodge

Frenchman Creek

Salmon River

Galena Summit

Owl Creek

Owl Creek Road

Prairie Creek

Prairie Creek Road

Gladiator Creek

Galena Lodge

Cherry Creek

Pole Creek Road

Baker Creek Road

Big Wood River

Silver Creek

Easley Hot Springs

BOULDER

MOUNTAINS

Boulder Creek

To Ketchum

N

0 1 2 3 4 MILE

116

45. The Harriman Trail

The Harriman Trail extends from the SNRA headquarters north of Ketchum all the way up to Galena Lodge. You can either ride up or down the trail, but don't be fooled into thinking it's gradual the entire way. This trail definitely has some ups and some downs.

Getting There: From Ketchum, drive north on Hwy 75 for 7.8 miles and turn right into the parking area for the SNRA headquarters. This is the end point of the ride. For a shuttle, leave a car here and continue driving up Hwy 75 for another 16.2 miles (24 miles total) and turn right into the Galena Lodge parking lot. Of course, you always start anywhere along the trail and go anywhere. Follow the signs, the ride begins here.
Length: 18.6 miles (one-way)
Starting Elevation: 7290'
Ending Elevation: 6280'
Total Elevation Loss: 1010'
The Ride: Anyway
Surface: 12' wide pea-gravel trail
Difficulty Rating: Easy/Moderate
Season: May - October
Fun Factor: Beautiful cruise up or down the valley following the Big Wood River and the Boulder Mountains all the way.
Summary: This ride is the perfect introductory ride for the person new to mountain biking or visiting the valley. Because of it's beautifully manicured terrain, you can enjoy this ride and still maintain a conversation. This could be classified as the perfect "first date" ride. No pressure to perform, no tears, good conversation . . .
The Ride: Start anywhere along the trail and enjoy!

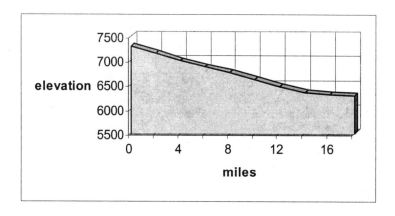

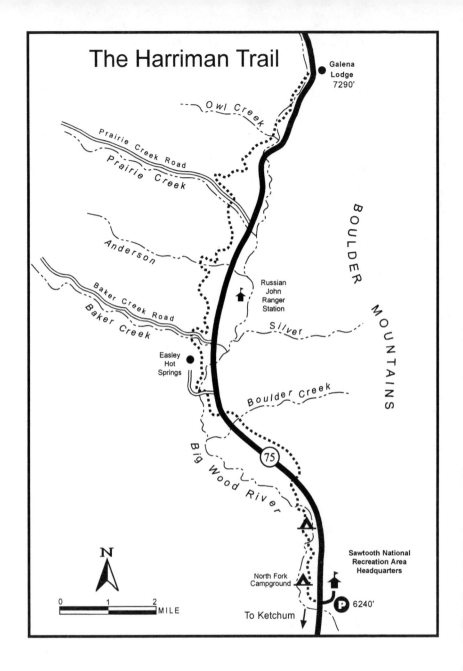

The Harriman Trail

Galena Lodge 7290'

Owl Creek

Prairie Creek Road

Prairie Creek

Anderson

BOULDER MOUNTAINS

Baker Creek Road

Baker Creek

Russian John Ranger Station

Silver

Easley Hot Springs

Boulder Creek

75

Big Wood River

Sawtooth National Recreation Area Headquarters

North Fork Campground

P 6240'

To Ketchum

N

0 1 2 MILE

46. Easley Loop (Curly's)

Length: 12.3 miles
Starting Elevation: 6675'
High Point Elevation: 8200'
Total Elevation Gain: 1525'
The Ride: Loop
Surface: Dirt jeep road and single track trail
Difficulty Rating: Moderate
Season: June - October
Fun Factor: Steady moderate climb to an outrageous downhill.
Summary: A gradual climb on a jeep road to a single track downhill that rivals any ride in the area.
Getting There: From Ketchum, drive north on Highway 75 approximately 15.5 miles and park on the right side of the road directly opposite of Baker Creek Road. The ride begins here.

Miles	The Ride:
0.0	From the parking area, cross back over the highway and begin riding up Baker Creek Road #162.
3.1	Just after crossing over the East Fork of Baker Creek, turn left onto the East Fork of Baker Creek Road #68 and begin a gradual climb.
5.1	At the fork, take the lower (left), more travelled road which descends for a bit before climbing again.
5.7	Another fork, take the right (upper), more travelled road and begin climbing another pitch.
6.3	Switchbacks, never too hard, but always a good get.
8.0	The saddle with a view and the top of the ride. Although the jeep road keeps going past this point, the top is marked by the end of the switchback and a small turn out on the left of the road next to a small tree. Great views to the west.
8.2	Whoa! While making a right turn on the road, look for the faint jeep trail leading off to the left which quickly becomes a great single-track descent heading down the ridgeline.
8.6	Pass by a watering hole and views of the Boulder Mountains.
10.7	Begin a rather steep descent down the ridgeline. Please avoid skidding here (or going over the bars for that matter), it has become a big problem. If you can't descend without skidding, think about walking your bike through this section.
11.5	The trail comes out next to some cabins, please don't bother the people here. Continue on the dirt roads paralleling the highway until riding onto the highway a couple hundred yards later.
11.7	Turn left onto Highway 75 and ride back to your car.
12.3	The end of the ride and back at the parking area.

Easley Loop

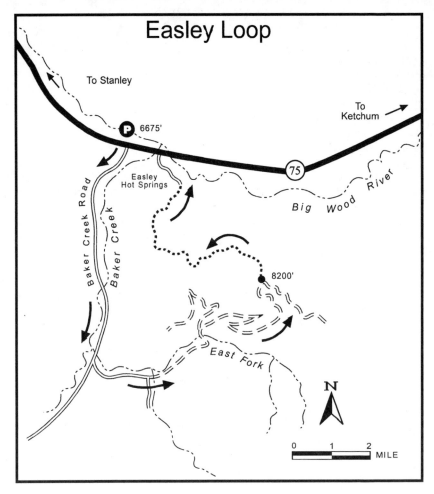

To Stanley

To Ketchum

P 6675'

Baker Creek Road

Baker Creek

Easley Hot Springs

75

Big Wood River

8200'

East Fork

N

| 0 | 1 | 2 | MILE |

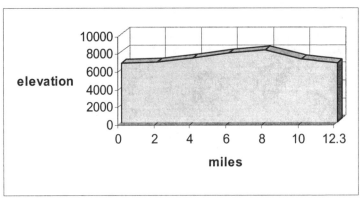

elevation

10000
8000
6000
4000
2000
0

0   2   4   6   8   10   12.3

miles

47. Baker Lake

Length: 3.4 miles
Starting Elevation: 7920'
High Point Elevation: 8800'
Total Elevation Gain: 880'
The Ride: Out and back
Surface: Single track trail
Difficulty Rating: Moderate
Season: June - October
Fun Factor: Short ride, alpine lake, killer views and many people.
Summary: If you are in the mood for a great quick ride in a gorgeous setting, this is the ride. It's short, weekends are crowded, but gives great views and the option for a swim in a nice warm mountain lake.
Getting There: From Ketchum, drive north on Hwy 75 for 15.5 miles and turn left onto Baker Creek Road. Continue up the dirt and gravel road for another 9.4 miles to the end of the road at the parking area. The ride begins here. (*This trail may become closed to mountain bikes in the near future, please obey any signs indicating this.)

<u>Miles</u>	<u>The Ride:</u>
0.0	Begin by riding across the small creek and grinding up a nice little incline. Don't fret, it slowly slacks off to a small grunt and casual switchbacks up to a saddle.
1.5	You'll soon reach a fork in the trail. The right fork leads to Apollo Creek and eventually to Norton Creek. Instead, stay left on the main trail to the lake.
1.7	Top of the ride. Take a swim, catch a fish and enjoy the surroundings. Turn around and follow your tracks back to the trailhead to complete the ride.
3.4	Back at your car and the end of the ride.

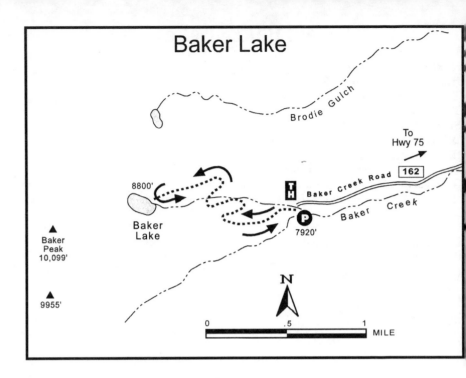

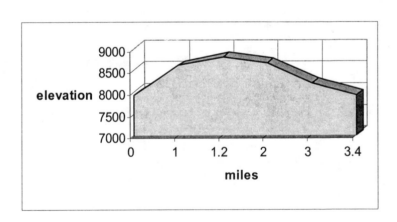

48. Baker Lake to Norton Creek

Length: 12.1 miles
Starting Elevation: 7300'
High Point Elevation: 9280'
Total Elevation Gain: 1980'
The Ride: Loop
Surface: Dirt jeep road and single track trail
Difficulty Rating: Difficult
Season: June - October
Fun Factor: Fun? Definitely. Adventurous? You know it.
Summary: This is also known as Apollo Creek Trail. This is a faith ride. Believe and you're in, don't, and you might as well not leave your car. Enjoy!
Getting There: From Ketchum, drive north on Hwy 75 for 15.5 miles and turn left onto Baker Creek Road. Continue on another 6 miles to the junction with Norton & Prairie Lakes Road and park on the right at the junction. The ride begins here. (*This trail may become closed to mountain bikes in the near future, please obey any signs indicating this.)

Miles	The Ride:
0.0	Begin by riding up Baker Creek Road heading south and up eventually to the Baker Lake parking area at the end of the road.
3.4	The Baker Lake parking area. Ride across the creek, register yourself and continue up the trail. The trail from here is not too steep but is still demanding.
4.9	Take the right fork leading off to Apollo Creek on trail #139. From here you'll do a traversing descent before grinding and pushing a bit. Here's the faith part of the ride. Follow the cairns and red tape attached to the trees. Pay attention, it's easy to miss them.
5.2	The trail disappears into the meadow. Stay in the dry creek bed, watching for the cairns leading to a tree 150 yards later where the trail reappears and switchbacks a bit before gaining a small saddle.
5.8	First saddle, walk down the scree and begin riding at the edge of the rocks following cairns and red tape for almost a mile.
6.5	Reach the dry creek bed of Apollo Creek. Continue up the other side to the fork in the trail. As the sign indicates, straight ahead is the Baker Lake Trail #138 and the right fork leads down into the Apollo Creek Trail #139. Stay straight traversing along the Baker Lake Trail.
7.3	Gain the saddle leading into the West Fork of Norton Creek drainage. This is where all the fun begins, a great trail and descent.
7.6	Fork in the trail. Turn right into the West Fork of Norton Creek drainage. A left turn here would lead into Bluff and Big Smoky Creeks in the South Fork of the Boise River drainage.
10.7	Junction with Norton Creek, Norton Lakes Trail #135 and the trailhead parking area. Ride across the creek, through the parking area and continue on down the jeep road to your car.
12.1	End of the ride.

Baker Lake to Norton Creek

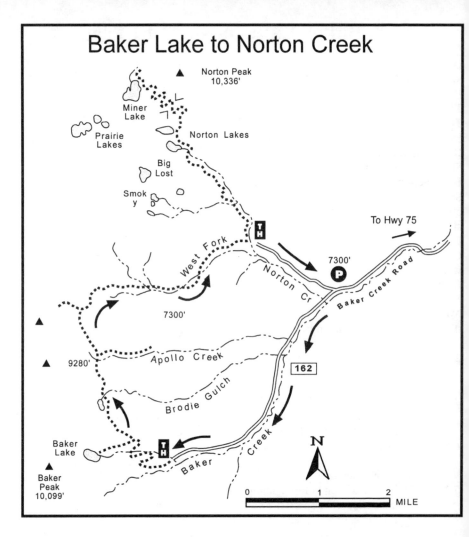

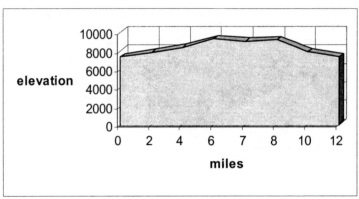

49. Prairie to Miner Loop

Length: 15.0 miles
Starting Elevation: 6900'
High Point Elevation: 8700'
Total Elevation Gain: 1800'
The Ride: Loop
Surface: Dirt jeep road and single track trail
Difficulty Rating: Moderate/Difficult
Season: June - October
Fun Factor: Lakes, creeks, mountains, and swimming.
Summary: Not only is this a great nordic skiing area, but the mountain biking here is phenomenal as well. Technical skills are helpful but not necessary, the grade is gradual and the scenery and swimming is even better!
Getting There: From Ketchum, drive north on Highway 75 for 18.5 miles to Prairie Creek Road. There is a big turn off next to the highway on the left. Park here, this is where the ride begins. (*You could also drive to the parking area at the end of Prairie Creek Road and begin there, saving an additional 2.6 miles.)

Miles	The Ride:
0.0	Begin by riding up the Prairie Creek Road which is both gravel, dirt and well traveled in the summertime.
2.6	Reach the trailhead for Prairie Lake and continue on with single track from this point just after crossing the creek. Buckle down and prepare for a continuous but moderate climb.
4.9	After some fun cruising up the valley and some gradual climbing, Minor Lake trail takes off on the left. Stay straight on the main trail up toward Prairie Lake, but make a note, this is where you will rejoin the trail later.
6.8	Encounter a small meadow with the creek running through it. Stay on the right side and cross over the creek at the upper end of the meadow and continue on to the lake.
7.2	Prairie Lake. Great swimming on the eastern side next to the trail. Careful of the creek flowing in, it's freezing! Look for the trail leading east away from the lake area. Follow this trail as it mostly contours it's way over to Miner Lake.
8.9	After rounding the top of the ridge, drop down into Miner Lake and join that trail down the valley.
10.1	Trail junction with the Prairie Lake Trail. Turn right and continue down to the trailhead.
12.4	The Prairie Lake Trailhead. If you parked here, great have a nice drive out, otherwise, continue down the gravel/dirt road to your car at Highway 75.
15.0	The end of the ride.

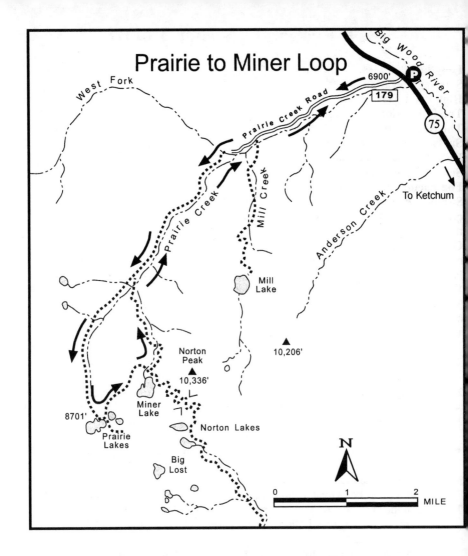

Prairie to Miner Loop

West Fork

Big Wood River

Prairie Creek Road

6900'

179

75

To Ketchum

Prairie Creek

Mill Creek

Anderson Creek

Mill Lake

10,206'

Norton Peak
10,336'

Miner Lake

8701'

Prairie Lakes

Big Lost

Norton Lakes

N

0   1   2
MILE

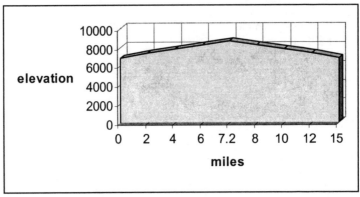

elevation

10000
8000
6000
4000
2000
0

0   2   4   6 7.2 8   10   12   15

miles

50. Owl Creek

Length: 7.2 miles
Starting Elevation: 7000'
High Point Elevation: 7900'
Total Elevation Gain: 900'
The Ride: Out and back
Surface: Dirt jeep road
Difficulty Rating: Easy/Moderate
Season: May - October
Fun Factor: Roller-coaster trail, killer downhill and beautiful views.
Summary: This is a fun, casual ride that can either be a date ride, a picnic ride or a quick aerobic workout before or after work. If you're feeling particularly amped, use this ride as a prelude to another ride close by (i.e. Galena Lodge Area Rides).
Getting There: From Ketchum, drive approximately 20.5 miles North on Hwy 75 until you see the Owl Creek turn off on the left. For reference, it is 2 miles past the Prarie Creek turn off. Turn left into the parking lot, this is where the ride begins.

Miles	The Ride:
0.0	Begin the ride by crossing the Big Wood River. Early season riders have been known to get washed back down the river to Ketchum so be careful here! Later in the season, the crossing comes as a relief to those finishing the ride in the heat of the day. Remember, this is a short ride, your climbing efforts are short lived.
2.1	Begin the start of a small series of hill climbs. Nothing too technical, but enough to keep the attention of your lungs and legs.
2.6	Enter a large meadow. Great views of Bromaghin Peak (elev. 10,225) ahead of you.
3.0	Begin a moderate climb that slacks off in .3 miles for a final ride to the trails end.
3.6	Elevation 7900' and the top of the ride. Be sure to catch the awesome views of the Boulder Mountains on the descent.
7.2	The end of the ride.

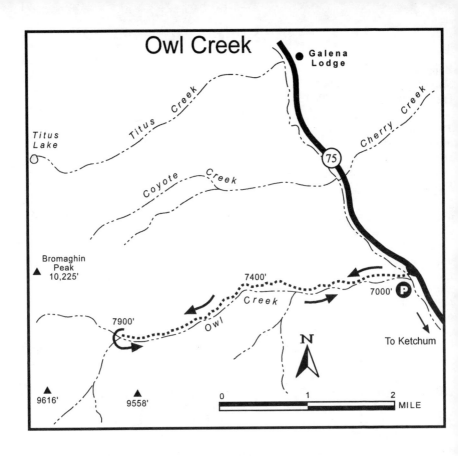

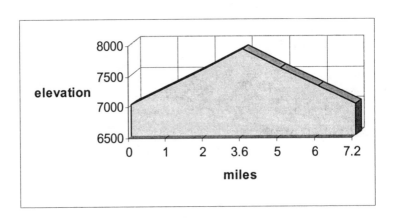

51. Galena Lodge Area Rides

Galena Lodge has been around since 1974 as a cross country skiing and mountain bike/hiking center. Since mountain biking and other outdoor recreation pursuits have increased in popularity over the years, the lodge has taken an aggressive move in creating a great trail network. With old mines and pioneer cabins throughout the area, any ride at Galena Lodge area is a great time. Maps are available for all the trails at the lodge, and the trails are well signed. Go up, have a great time and enjoy a lunch or dinner on the deck in the heart of the Sawtooth National Recreation Area.

Getting There: From Ketchum, drive north on Hwy 75 for 24 miles until you see the Galena Lodge sign and lodge on the right side of the road. Turn right into the parking lot to begin your fun. If you reach Galena Summit, you've gone too far, but will have an awesome view of the Sawtooth and Boulder Mountains in return.

Grinder Trail

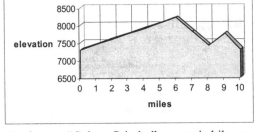

Length: 10 miles
Starting Elevation: 7290'
High Point Elevation: 8200'
Total Elevation Gain: 1090'
The Ride: Loop
Surface: Single track trail
Difficulty Rating: Difficult
Season: June - September

Fun Factor: This is the same ride as the famous "Galena Grinder" mountain bike race course. The name "Grinder" should be a clue.

Summary: Starting with a cruiser up the Senate Meadow, you then climb up the jeep road to a single track trail traversing the mountains all the way down into the gulch by the corrals after passing straight through the gravel pit. From here the trail climbs up and over the hill down into Gladiator Meadow and back to Galena Lodge.

Psycho Trail

Length: 4.8 miles
Starting Elevation: 7290'
High Point Elevation: 7750'
Total Elevation Gain: 460'
The Ride: Loop
Surface: Single track trail
Difficulty Rating: Difficult
Season: June - September

Fun Factor: Quick and steep (not too bad). A great warm-up.

Summary: With a nice gradual warm up riding through Gladiator Meadow, you turn left and begin a gradual climb up to the top of Westernhome Gulch. From here you turn left again following the ridgeline down and back to Galena Lodge in time for lunch.

Rip & Tear Trail

Length: 4.5 miles
Starting Elevation: 7290'
High Point Elevation: 7800'
Total Elevation Gain: 510'
The Ride: Loop
Surface: Single track trail
Difficulty Rating: Moderate
Season: June - September

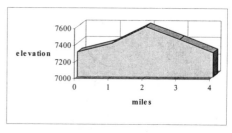

Fun Factor: Another short, but sweet loop.
Summary: Begin with another gradually climbing warm-up through Gladiator Meadow. At the Forest Service sign showing the Grinder Connector Trail turning left, you turn right and begin climbing some switchbacks to the top. Once topped out, start traversing the mountainside before dropping down into Senate Meadow and back to Galena Lodge.

Galena Loop

Length: 4 miles
Starting Elevation: 7290'
High Point Elevation: 7600''
Total Elevation Gain: 310'
The Ride: Loop
Surface: Single track trail
Difficulty Rating: Easy
Season: June - September

Fun Factor: A great, fun warm-up to what Sun Valley mountain biking is all about.
Summary: With a fun cruise up through Senate Meadows, turn right just after the Senate Creek Smelter and continue past the trail leading off left into Cherry Creek. After a fun downhill, pass by the Galena Pioneer Cemetary on the right and eventually back to the highway. From here, ride up the road to Galena Lodge or back-track the same way you came from.

Galena Lodge Rides

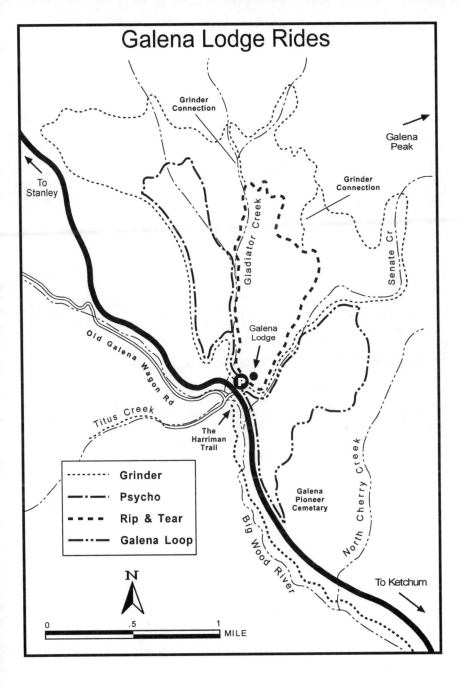

Grinder Connection

Galena Peak

Grinder Connection

To Stanley

Gladiator Creek

Senate Cr

Old Galena Wagon Rd

Galena Lodge

P

Titus Creek

The Harriman Trail

Grinder
Psycho
Rip & Tear
Galena Loop

Galena Pioneer Cemetary

North Cherry Creek

Big Wood River

To Ketchum

N

0   .5   1
MILE

Another typical day in the Sawtooth Mountains
Courtesy of the McBob Collection

52. Salmon River Headwaters

Length: 10.6 miles
Starting Elevation: 7350'
High Point Elevation: 7780'
Total Elevation Gain: 430'
The Ride: Out and back
Surface: Dirt jeep road
Difficulty Rating: Easy
Season: May - October
Fun Factor: Gorgeous canyon setting with an abundance of wildlife.
Summary: If you are looking for an incredible cruiser for anytime of the day or night, this is the ultimate. Gorgeous views, wildlife and stream crossings make this a classic ride along the headwaters of the famous Salmon River.
Getting There: From Main Street in Ketchum, drive north on Highway 75 over Galena Summit to the parking area approximately 34.5 miles away. Turn left onto road #215 and park anywhere close by. From Stanley, drive south on Highway 75 for approximately 27 miles to the turn off. The ride begins here.

Miles	The Ride:
0.0	Begin by riding south on the dirt jeep road, a bit washboarded at times.
0.9	Road junction. Stay right on the main road with a sign pointing to "Chemeketan Campground." The road to the left goes up to the top of Galena Summit.
2.4	Again, you will come to a few spur roads, stay on the main road.
2.7	The canyon closes in and opens up again, then you encounter an incredible view of a meadow in front of you. In early season, you may have a colorful display of wildflowers.
3.2	Chemeketan Campground, a great place to have a picnic on the way up or down. Stay on the main road, crossing the stream and continuing up the canyon.
4.9	Stream crossing here and another one in .2 miles.
5.3	Top of the ride. This is where the trail divides. You can either turn around here or by taking the left fork you can eventually reach Big Smoky Creek and Skillern Hot Springs. If you continue on up the trail, be prepared, it is a very long ride out and a shuttle is the best way. If turning around here you have got a great downhill ride ahead of you.
10.6	The end of the ride.

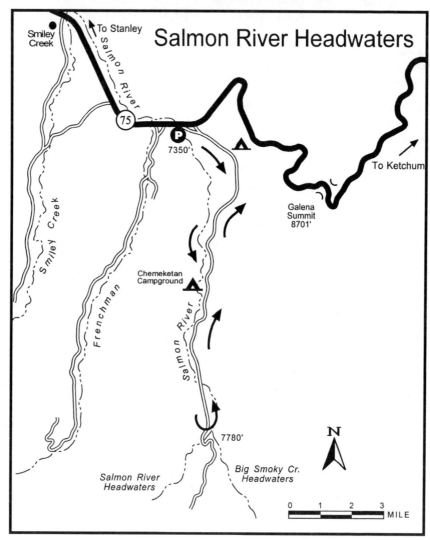

Salmon River Headwaters

Smiley Creek

To Stanley

Salmon River

75

P
7350'

Galena Summit
8701'

To Ketchum

Smiley Creek

Frenchman

Chemeketan Campground

Salmon River

N

7780'

Salmon River Headwaters

Big Smoky Cr. Headwaters

0 1 2 3 MILE

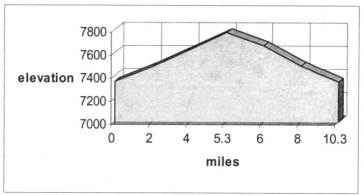

elevation

53. Frenchman Creek

Length: 10.8 miles
Starting Elevation: 7240'
High Point Elevation: 7780'
Total Elevation Gain: 540'
The Ride: Out and back
Surface: Dirt jeep road
Difficulty Rating: Easy/Moderate
Season: May - October
Fun Factor: Another fun filled canyon with beautiful views and wildlife.
Summary: This is another one of those moderate elevation gain, out and back canyon cruisers for the photographic at heart. This is most incredible in the morning and early evening hours.
Getting There: From Main Street in Ketchum, drive north on Highway 75, up and over Galena Summit, just past milepost 163, 35.2 miles away. Turn out on the left and park near the highway at the trailhead, road #195. From Stanley, drive south on Highway 75 for approximately 26.5 miles to the turn off. The ride begins here.

Miles	The Ride:
0.0	Begin by taking the right or west fork staying on the main road passing a sign telling you to stay on designated roads. The first 2 miles of this ride are rolling and climb a bit, but eventually open up to a huge gorgeous valley.
0.7	A spur road, stay on the main road.
0.8	Another spur road and camping area, but stay on the main road going next to the creek and eventually crossing it.
1.5	Encounter an Idaho Fish and Game Wild Trout Management Area.
4.1	Begin climbing up a moderate hill, never too steep and always rideable.
4.5	Top of the climb with a "danger" sign on the spur road to the right. Stay on the main road continuing on up the valley.
4.9	Check out the old cabins on the right.
5.4	This is the top of the ride. The road crosses over a small creek and begins to go up the canyon to the west. The road from here climbs steeply to a sheep herders camp and across the mountainside to a viewpoint possibly reached only by a few hearty riders and aerobic seeking hikers. Turn around here and enjoy the awesome downhill ride back to your car.
10.8	The end of the ride.

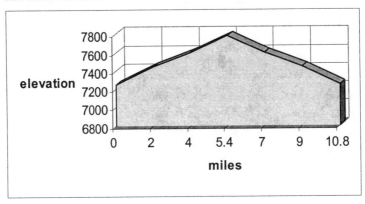

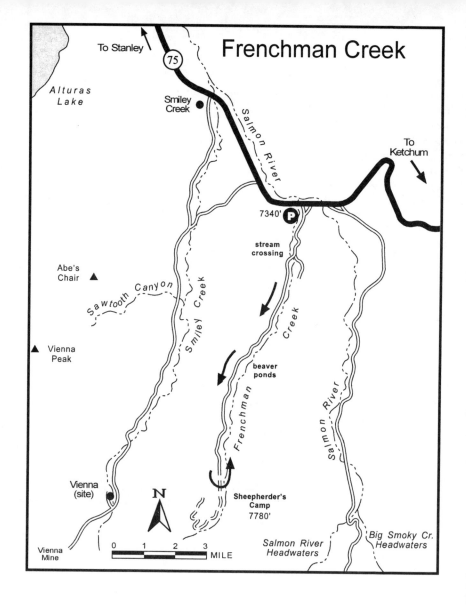

To Stanley

75

Frenchman Creek

Alturas
Lake

Smiley
Creek

Salmon River

To
Ketchum

7340' **P**

stream
crossing

Abe's
Chair ▲

Sawtooth Canyon

Smiley Creek

Frenchman Creek

beaver
ponds

▲ Vienna
Peak

Salmon River

Vienna
(site)

N

Sheepherder's
Camp
7780'

0 1 2 3
MILE

Vienna
Mine

Salmon River
Headwaters

Big Smoky Cr.
Headwaters

54. Smiley Creek (Vienna)

Length: 13.2 miles
Starting Elevation: 6750'
High Point Elevation: 7550'
Total Elevation Gain: 800'
The Ride: Out and back
Surface: Dirt jeep road
Difficulty Rating: Easy/Moderate
Season: May - October
Fun Factor: Alpine meadows, rocky peaks and the historic mining town of Vienna.
Summary: Anytime of the day makes this a great ride through beautiful alpine meadows following Smiley Creek up to the historic mining town of Vienna. Exploring the area is a must if you have the time.
Getting There: From Ketchum, drive north on Highway 75 up and over Galena Summit to the turn off on the left for Smiley Creek Road, approximately 35 miles (this is before you reach Smiley Creek Lodge). Turn left onto the dirt road and park. If coming from Stanley, drive south on Highway 75 for just over 25.5 miles and turn right onto the road. The ride begins here.

Miles	The Ride:
0.0	Begin by riding up the dirt road heading in a southwestern direction.
1.5	A spur road on the right leads to Sawtooth City, stay on the main road following Smiley Creek.
2.0	The road begins cruising next to some beautiful grassy alpine meadows.
6.2	Buckle down and prepare to begin some small and fairly steep sections.
6.6	The top of the ride and welcome to the townsite of Vienna. Do some exploring, but please don't take anything home with you. If you choose to be adventurous, continue on up the road and you'll eventually encounter Emma Creek, Paradise Creek or the North Fork of Big Smoky Creek, all of which will take you down to the South Fork of the Boise River drainage. But instead, you'll probably want to reach the comfort of your car eventually, so turn around here for a very fun downhill.
13.2	The end of the ride.

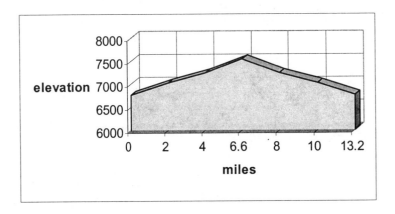

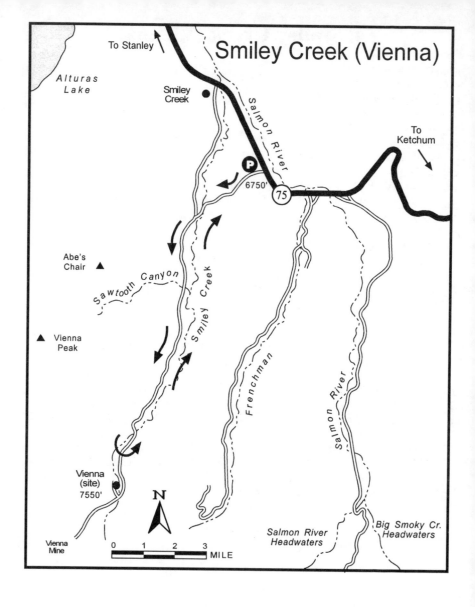

Smiley Creek (Vienna)

To Stanley

Alturas Lake

Smiley Creek

Salmon River

To Ketchum

P
6750'

75

Abe's Chair ▲

Sawtooth Canyon

▲ Vienna Peak

Smiley Creek

Frenchman

Salmon River

Vienna (site) 7550'

N

Vienna Mine

0 1 2 3 MILE

Salmon River Headwaters

Big Smoky Cr. Headwaters

55. The Bowery Loop

Length: 30.5 miles
Starting Elevation: 7760'
High Point Elevation: 9060'
Total Elevation Gain: 4670'
The Ride: Loop
Surface: Dirt jeep road and single-track
Difficulty Rating: Abusive/Gonzo
Season: July - September

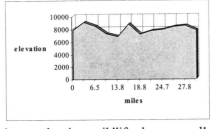

Fun Factor: Remote wilderness area with views and serious wildlife...be prepared!

Summary: You'll feel good at the top of Grand Prize Gulch, you'll even feel good by the time you reach Bowery. But by the time you reach the top of the hike-a-bike, you'll be praying to the Endurance Gods for forgiveness. The rest is a classic wilderness ride.

Getting There: From Ketchum, drive north on Highway 75 for just over 37 miles and turn right at the sign pointing the way to "Pole Creek Road and Valley Road." (If you go flying past the Smiley Creek Lodge, you've just gone 0.5 miles too far) If coming from Stanley, go south on Highway 75 for just over 24.5 miles and turn left at the same sign. Stay on the main road heading toward the mountains, passing several spur roads along the way. At 2.3 miles on this road, you cross over Pole Creek and come to a junction. Continue forward on the road heading toward "Germania Basin." The left fork becomes Valley Road. Follow this road for another 4.2 miles to Grand Prize Gulch appears on the right. The ride begins and ends here.

Miles	The Ride:
0.0	Begin by finding the trail which crosses over Pole Creek. Just after crossing the creek, be sure to take the left fork 0.3 miles later.
1.5	The road ends at the creek crossing and becomes single-track.
2.9	The switchbacks end in high alpine meadows.
3.7	Just after the main saddle, Gladiator Trail takes off on the right.
9.0	Small junction with the West Fork and South Fork. Stay on the main trail.
11.4	Cross by sign showing Ibex Creek canyon on the right.
12.6	A small trail takes off to the left. Both trails get to the same place, but stay right and cross the creek.
13.4	Gate, please close.
13.6	Take the very faint trail which cuts back to the left just when the guard station comes into view. Follow this trail down to the bridge that crosses over the creek by the guard station. Go through the guard station courtyard area to the gate against the hill on the west side. Close the gate behind you and go right.
14.0	Another gate crossing, keep traversing the hillside before starting the hike-a-bike climbing section in the aspen trees ahead of you.
14.6	The climbing seriously begins now, either push, carry or cry.
16.6	Yes! This is the top, nice job! Scramble up the 9059' peak on the right for killer views of Castle Peak. Careful going down from here, it is seriously loose, steep and dangerous. If you get hurt here, you are a long ways from help!
18.8	The trail intersects Germania Creek, stay left.
19.7	Yes, cross the creek here, anywhere you can and continue riding left and up.
23.2	Junction with Washington Lakes/Chamberlain Lakes Trail. Stay on main trail.
24.7	End of the single-track and junction with Pole Creek Road. Ride up the road.
27.8	The top of Pole Creek Summit. It's all downhill from here!
30.5	End of the ride and back at your car.

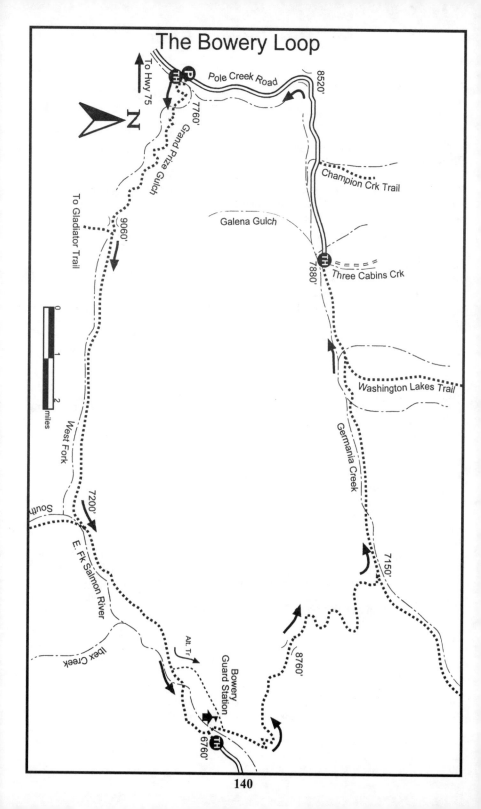

The Bowery Loop

To Hwy 75

Pole Creek Road

8520'

TH

P

7760'

Grand Prize Gulch

N

Champion Crk Trail

Galena Gulch

9060'

To Gladiator Trail

7880'

TH

Three Cabins Crk

Washington Lakes Trail

West Fork

Germania Creek

0 1 2 miles

7200'

South

E. Fk Salmon River

7150'

Ibex Creek

Alt. Tr.

Bowery Guard Station

8760'

6760'

TH

56. Pole Creek

Length: 10.6 miles
Starting Elevation: 7400'
High Point Elevation: 8550'
Total Elevation Gain: 1150'
The Ride: Out and back
Surface: Dirt jeep road
Difficulty Rating: Moderate/Difficult
Season: June - October
Fun Factor: The views of Sawtooth and White Cloud Mountains, the creeks, and the wildlife.
Summary: What looks like a rather hum-drum ride quickly turns into a lesson in photography as you want to take a picture around every turn. The high White Cloud Mountains are like no other.
Getting There: From Ketchum, drive north on Highway 75 for just over 37 miles and turn right at the sign pointing the way to "Pole Creek Road and Valley Road." (If you go flying past the Smiley Creek Lodge, you've just gone 0.5 miles too far) If coming from Stanley, go south on Highway 75 for just over 24.5 miles and turn left at the same sign. Stay on the main road heading toward the mountains, passing several spur roads along the way. At 2.3 miles on this road, you cross over Pole Creek and come to a junction. Continue forward on the road heading toward "Germania Basin." The left fork becomes Valley Road. At 3.7 miles in from the highway, there are some corrals on the right. Park anywhere near here and begin the ride.

Miles	The Ride:
0.0	Begin by riding on the main dirt road heading in toward the trees. Stay left at the first fork.
0.9	After passing by several spur roads, pass by the Twin Creek Trail #107 on the left.
2.6	You'll pass by three more spur roads, stay on the main road at all times. Then Grand Prize Trail #112 exits off to the right. Stay on the main road as it meanders through the trees climbing steadily as it goes.
4.1	This is a great part of the ride where you enter into the "saddle corridor." Slowing climbing up the saddle overlooking the valleys below as you go.
5.3	Gain the saddle and giant meadow which slowly drops into Germania Creek. This is the top of the ride, now enjoy the downhill back to your car.
10.6	End of the ride.

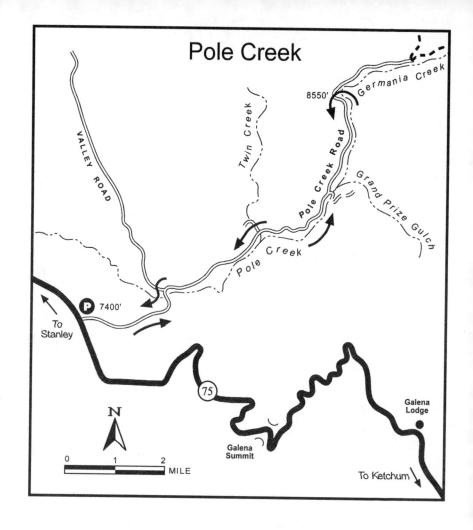

Pole Creek

Twin Creek

Germania Creek

8550'

VALLEY ROAD

Pole Creek Road

Grand Prize Gulch

Pole Creek

P 7400'

To Stanley

75

N

Galena Lodge

Galena Summit

To Ketchum

0   1   2
MILE

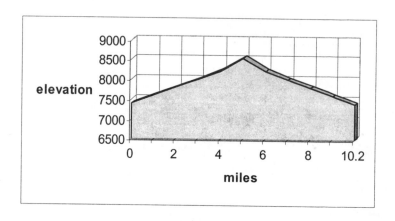

elevation

9000
8500
8000
7500
7000
6500

0   2   4   6   8   10.2

miles

57. Sawtooth City

Length: 6 miles
Starting Elevation: 7165'
High Point Elevation: 7365'
Total Elevation Gain: 200'
The Ride: Loop
Surface: Dirt jeep road
Difficulty Rating: Easy
Season: May - October
Fun Factor: Fun, historic mining site and a cruiser ride.
Summary: For a regional history lesson and a mountain bike ride all in one, may we present Sawtooth City. With cabin ruins all around the city, take some time to explore a bit of this fine historic area. Please don't take anything home with you.
Getting There: From Ketchum, drive north on Hwy 75 for 37.5 miles and just about a mile past the Smiley Creek Lodge to Beaver Creek Rd #204 and park at the pull out on the left of the highway. This is approximately 23.5 miles south on Highway 75 from Stanley. You will see a "Historic Landmark" sign giving the history of Sawtooth City. The ride begins on the south end of this highway pull-out.

Miles	The Ride:
0.0	Begin by crossing the cattle guard and riding up the dirt road next to Beaver Creek.
0.6	After crossing the cattle guard, the road forks, stay straight on the left fork here.
0.9	Continue forward passing spur roads on each side of the main trail.
1.0	More spur roads and camping areas. Stay straight on the main trail following Beaver Creek.
1.9	Major road junction here. Stay on the main road passing a "beautiful forest" sign. If you take the right fork here, you'll climb a short hill and come to the historic town cemetery. (As you look toward the creek, you'll see why they call it Beaver Creek).
2.2	Welcome to Sawtooth City and the top of the ride. Take some time to explore the area. From here you turn around and head back down the valley. If you want to explore a bit further, the road past Sawtooth City continues on up the valley and ends at 6.8 miles at the Silver King and Pilgrim Mines. Be careful there, mining shafts can collapse at anytime.
2.5	Once you've turned around at Sawtooth City and started heading down, you encounter the same main junction as you did on the way up. From here, you can either head back down the main trail to the highway and trailhead, or make a loop of it as the map shows.
	Loop: Turn right at the main junction here and down a small hill to the creek. Cross the creek (be careful in early Springtime) and continue down the dirt road for approximately 1 mile and turn left on another faint dirt road. This road will take you out to Highway 75 close to the Beaver Creek store. Continue down the side of the highway on a dirt trail (west side), but not before examining the interesting wood works outside the store.
6.0	End of the ride.

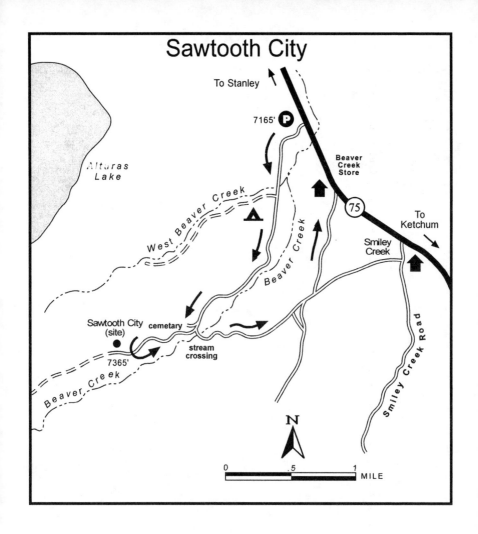

Sawtooth City

To Stanley

7165' **P**

Alturas Lake

West Beaver Creek

Beaver Creek Store

75

To Ketchum

Smiley Creek

Sawtooth City (site)

cemetary

7365'

stream crossing

Beaver Creek

Smiley Creek Road

N

0 .5 1 MILE

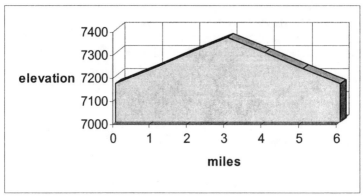

elevation

7400
7300
7200
7100
7000

0 1 2 3 4 5 6

miles

58. Alturas Lake Creek

Length: 8.0 miles
Starting Elevation: 7050'
High Point: 7120'
Elevation Gain: 70'
The Ride: Out and back
Surface: Pavement and dirt jeep road
Difficulty Rating: Easy
Season: April - October
Fun Factor: Beautiful introductory ride to the Sawtooth Valley with casual riding, wildlife viewing and a lake to cool off in.
Summary: If you want a casual ride in the Sawtooths that is incredibly gorgeous in the mornings and late afternoons, this is an excellent choice. In the early springtime the wildflowers are amazing, as are the views of the Sawtooth Mountain range.
Getting There: From Ketchum Main Street, drive north on highway 75 over top of Galena Summit to the Alturas Lake turnoff (road #205), approximately 40.5 miles. It is also just over 21 miles south on Highway 75 from Stanley. Turning left onto Alturas Lake Road, drive 2.4 miles to the second picnic area B and park. The ride begins here.

Miles	The Ride:
0.0	Begin by riding up the road around Alturas Lake. Be careful in the mid-summer months due to excessive tourist traffic.
1.0	Pass by Smokey Bear Campground and continue on the main road heading west following the contour of the lake.
2.8	The road passes by Inlet Campground. Stay on the main road heading up the canyon following Alturas Lake Creek. From here the road roller-coasters a bit, never gaining or losing much elevation.
4.0	The road takes an abrupt halt at the creek. This is the top of the ride. On the left is Eureka Gulch and on the right is Alpine Creek trailhead. If you want to continue up Alpine Creek, you can only go about 1 mile before coming to the wilderness area boundary which doesn't allow bicycles beyond that point. If you want a bit more of an adventure, continue on up the main road for approximately 4.5 miles before it becomes a bit steep and more like a hiking trail. Enjoy the downhill ride back to your car at the picnic area.
8.0	The end of the ride.

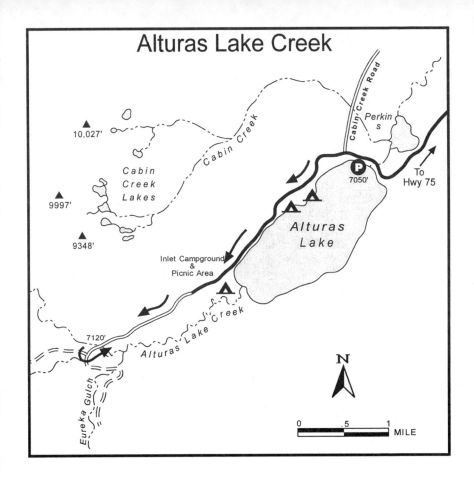

Alturas Lake Creek

10,027'

Cabin Creek

Cabin Creek Lakes

9997'

9348'

Inlet Campground & Picnic Area

7120'

Alturas Lake Creek

Eureka Gulch

Cabin Creek Road

Perkins

P 7050'

To Hwy 75

Alturas Lake

N

0   .5   1
MILE

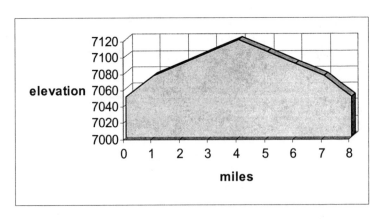

elevation

7120
7100
7080
7060
7040
7020
7000

0 1 2 3 4 5 6 7 8

miles

59. Alturas Lake To Pettit Lake

Length: 11.4 miles
Starting Elevation: 7050'
High Point Elevation: 7100'
Total Elevation Gain: 50'
The Ride: Out and back
Surface: Dirt jeep road
Difficulty Rating: Easy
Season: April - October
Fun Factor: Great views, wildlife and wildflowers.
Summary: Okay, let's say you want to tour the Sawtooth Valley with an easy ride, well, here you go. This is the perfect picnic ride. Pack your wine and cheese (don't forget the Swiss Army Knife), and ride through the sagebrush meadows looking for wildlife and early season wildflowers.
Getting There: From Ketchum, drive north on Highway 75 over top of Galena Summit to the Alturas Lake turnoff (road #205), approximately 40.5 miles. It is also just over 21 miles south on Highway 75 from Stanley. Turning left onto Alturas Lake Road, drive 2.4 miles to the second picnic area B and park here.

Miles	The Ride:
0.0	Begin by continuing to ride up Alturas Lake Creek Road heading west.
0.3	Turn right on Road #207 Cabin Creek Road.
0.7	Cabins and a faint trail are off to the right. Stay on the main Cabin Creek Road ignoring a few small spur roads off to the left over the next half mile.
1.5	A jeep trail is off to the right, but continue on the main road and climb a little bit before leveling off.
2.1	Look carefully and turn right onto a faint trail paralleling the powerlines which quickly pass a spur road on the right which begins to veer away from the powerlines and around behind a rock outcropping. The faint road now begins to follow the creek weaving in and out of the trees. Yes, this is the trail, stay on it and have faith!
3.3	Pass a spur road on the right and another on the left followed shortly by a corral on the left.
3.7	Meet up with Cabin Creek Road again. Do not turn to the right and cross the bridge over Alturas Lake Creek. Cross over the road and slightly left, cruise through the trees, and eventually around the fence.
4.8	The infamous sheep bridge over Vat Creek. Take a picture, it'll last longer. After the bridge is a 3-way intersection, follow the center choice which goes up and over the ridge into Pettit Lake.
5.4	A three-way intersection at Pettit Lake. We always go to the "Day Use Area".
5.7	The top of the ride at Pettit Lake. Take a swim and enjoy exploring around the area. When you are ready to leave, follow your same route on the return trip. There are several roads which lead back to Alturas Lake, so choosing any of them you can't really go wrong.
11.4	End of the ride.

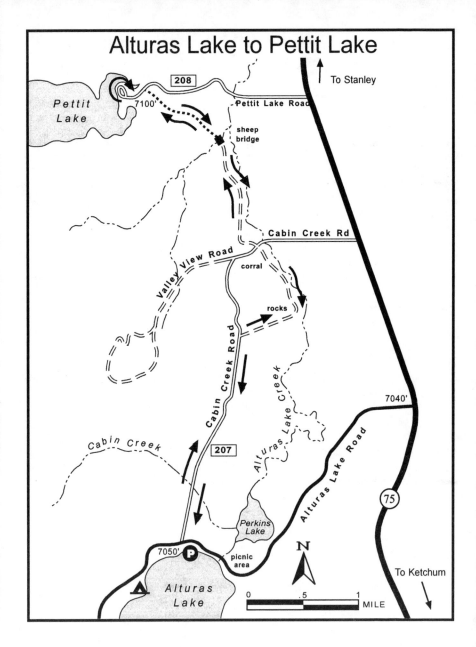

Alturas Lake to Pettit Lake

Pettit Lake

208

7100'

Pettit Lake Road

To Stanley

sheep bridge

Cabin Creek Rd

Valley View Road

corral

rocks

Cabin Creek Road

207

Cabin Creek

Alturas Lake Creek

Alturas Lake Road

7040'

75

Perkins Lake

picnic area

N

7050'

P

7050'

Alturas Lake

To Ketchum

0   .5   1
MILE

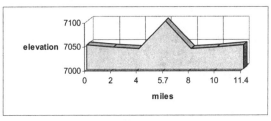

elevation

7100

7050

7000

0   2   4   5.7   8   10   11.4

miles

Canoeing the Salmon River outside Stanley, circa 1940

Courtesy of Community Library, Ketchum, Idaho, Regional History Department

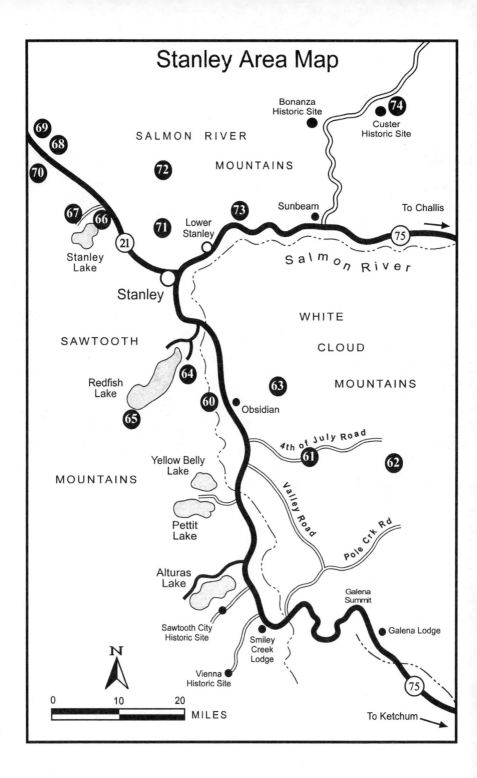

Stanley Area Map

60. Decker Flats Road

Length: 14.9 miles
Starting Elevation: 6775'
High Point Elevation: 6570'
Total Elevation Gain: 205'
The Ride: One-way
Surface: Dirt jeep road and pavement
Difficulty Rating: Easy
Season: April - October
Fun Factor: Incredible views and wildlife
Summary: This is an amazingly beautiful ride for evenings or early mornings with wildflowers, wildlife and the wild Sawtooth Mountains looming over the trees to the west.
Getting There: From Ketchum, drive north 47.5 miles on Highway 75 over Galena Summit, past Smiley Creek Lodge and Fourth of July Creek Road to Decker Flat Road #210. Turn left here. Cross over the Salmon River shortly and park on the right near the campground next to the river. This trailhead is approximately 15 miles south on Highway 75 from Stanley. The ride begins here. (To shuttle a car to the end of the ride, continue driving north on Highway 75 to Redfish Lake Road. Follow this road approximately 2 miles and turn right on Road #213 to the lodge next to the lake.

Miles	The Ride:
0.0	Begin riding from Hell Roaring Creek campground (aka Surf City) and ride north on the main dirt jeep road contouring the foothills and trees.
0.5	The road splits and follows a small canal, take the right side road.
0.9	The road splits again, take the left fork.
1.1	Deja vu, the road splits again, take the left fork and notice the incredible views of the Sawtooths.
1.6	The road splits here, take the left fork.
1.8	Then the road takes a turn to the right.
2.5	Turn right on the road away from the fence.
2.6	Cross a faint dirt road, but stay straight for another tenth of a mile.
2.7	Intersection with Decker Flats Road. Turn left here.
5.4	The road crosses over a small creek.
6.6	Surprise, another spur road off to the left, stay right on the main road.
7.3	After climbing a fairly small hill, you begin a gradual descent.
8.3	Climb again and top out at 6775'.
9.2	Encounter a huge meadow on the left (natures beauty at its best).
11.9	Intersection. Stay on the left road with cabins on the right.
13.0	Intersection with Redfish Lake Road and pavement. Turn left here, but be careful, the road is very busy.
14.5	Whoa! Easy turn to miss. Turn right on road #213 to Redfish Lake Lodge.
14.9	The end of your ride at Redfish Lake Lodge. The water is a bit cool, but perfect after this ride with plenty of other things to do there as well.

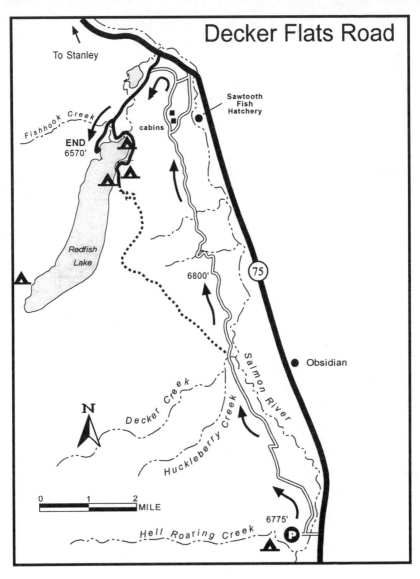

Decker Flats Road

To Stanley

Fishhook Creek

Sawtooth
Fish
Hatchery

cabins

END
6570'

Redfish
Lake

6800'

75

N

Decker Creek

Obsidian

Salmon River

Huckleberry Creek

0   1   2
MILE

Hell Roaring Creek

6775'

P

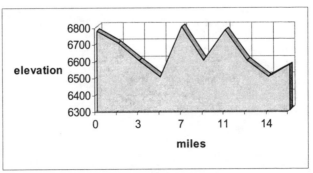

elevation

6800
6700
6600
6500
6400
6300

0   3   7   11   14

miles

154

61. Fourth of July Creek

Length: 25.6 miles
Starting Elevation: 6800'
High Point Elevation: 9580'
Total Elevation Gain: 2780'
The Ride: Out and back
Surface: Dirt jeep road and single track trail
Difficulty Rating: Moderate/Difficult
Season: June - October
Fun Factor: High mountain lakes and the White Cloud Mountains.
Summary: What starts as a mellow gradual climbing ride turns into a bit of a grind near the top of the road and great cruising through mountain meadows around the lakes. **Getting There:** From Ketchum, drive north 47 miles on Highway 75 over Galena Summit, past Smiley Creek Lodge to Fourth of July Creek Road. Turn right here and park anywhere in the sage by the road. This road is approximately 15 miles from Stanley by heading south on Highway 75.

<u>Miles</u>	<u>The Ride</u>:
0.0	Begin by riding up the dirt/gravel road heading east toward the White Cloud Mountains.
1.0	Pass by the Fourth of July Creek Ranch on the right.
1.7	Enter in the trees by the creek. From here, the road winds while climbing gradually through the trees following the creek.
4.1	Cabin ruins and white cliffs on the left.
4.8	Pass by Champion Creek Trailhead on the right.
8.3	A primitive campground on the right marks the beginning of more "aggressive climbing" to come. Gear down.
9.2	A slight break from climbing in the meadows.
10.3	Trailhead. Please register to make the USFS happy. From here, follow the single track trail to the two lakes ahead.
10.5	At the junction, cross the road and continue on the single track trail.
11.8	Another trail junction. The left fork leads over the saddle and into Warm Springs Creek eventually joining up with Fisher Creek (very adventurous). Instead, take the right (forward) fork and come to Fourth of July Lake just ahead of you. From here continue on the right or west side of the lake and up the trail to the saddle with Washington Lake.
12.3	The saddle with Washington Lake is one-half mile ahead.
12.8	You've reached Washington Lake and the top of the ride. It's a long way back home, be careful and wear your helmet!
25.6	The end of the ride.

Fourth of July Creek

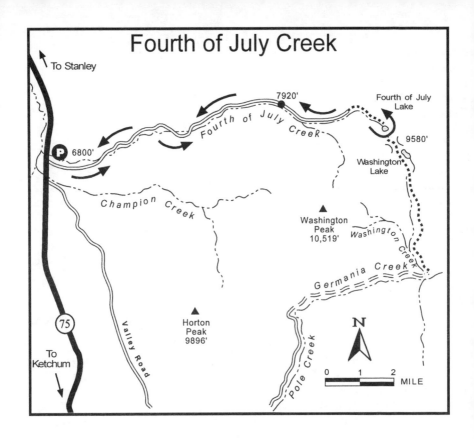

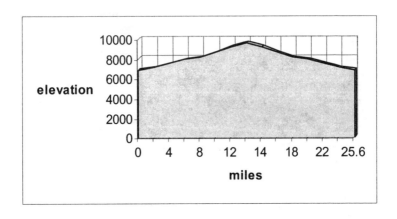

62. Fourth of July to Pole Creek

Length: 38.1 miles
Starting Elevation: 6800'
High Point Elevation: 9580'
Total Elevation Gain: 2780'
The Ride: Loop
Surface: Dirt road and single track trail
Difficulty Rating: Difficult/Abusive
Season: June - October

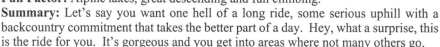

Fun Factor: Alpine lakes, great descending and fun climbing.

Summary: Let's say you want one hell of a long ride, some serious uphill with a backcountry commitment that takes the better part of a day. Hey, what a surprise, this is the ride for you. It's gorgeous and you get into areas where not many others go.

Getting There: From Ketchum, drive north 47 miles on Highway 75 over Galena Summit past Smiley Creek Lodge to Fourth of July Creek Road. Turn right here and park anywhere in the sage by the road. This road is approximately 15 miles from Stanley by heading south on Highway 75. The ride begins here.

<u>Miles</u>	<u>The Ride</u>:
0.0	Begin by riding up the dirt/gravel road heading east toward the White Cloud Mountains.
1.0	Pass by the Fourth of July Creek Ranch on the right.
1.7	Enter in the trees by the creek. From here, the road winds while climbing gradually through the trees following the creek.
4.1	Cabin ruins and white cliffs on the left.
4.8	Pass by Champion Creek Trailhead on the right.
8.3	A primitive campground on the right marks the beginning of more "aggressive climbing" to come. Gear down.
9.2	A slight break from climbing in the meadows.
10.3	Trailhead. Please register to make the USFS happy. From here, follow the single track trail to the two lakes ahead.
11.8	Trail junction. The left fork leads over the saddle and into Warm Springs Creek eventually joining up with Fisher Creek (very adventurous). Instead, take the right (forward) fork and come to Fourth of July Lake just ahead of you. From here continue on to the lake and up the trail to the saddle with Washington Lake.
12.8	You've reached Washington Lake. Continue on the trail as it descends into Germania Creek.
13.6	At the fork, turn right heading toward Germania Creek where it climbs a short bit before becoming more mellow a half mile later.
15.9	At the fork, turn left and down toward Germania Creek, heading toward the junction of Germania and Washington Creeks.
16.7	Another fork, stay straight (right) and continue riding down a steep section into Germania Creek.
17.6	Trail junction: Join Germania Creek Trail and turn right here climbing slightly up to the main road.
18.9	The Germania Creek Trailhead. Follow the road up and out for the next 3 miles ascending the upper Germania Creek drainage.
22.1	The top of Pole Creek summit.

28.6   Whoa! At the junction, be careful not to miss the right turn here leading up the small hill on Valley Road. Continue on Valley Road all the way to Hwy 75, cruising down the east side of the Salmon River basin.

37.6   End of Valley Road and junction with Hwy 75. Turn right here and continue heading north down Hwy 75 to Fourth of July Creek Road.

38.1   Turn right on Fourth of July Creek Road and return to your car. This is the end.

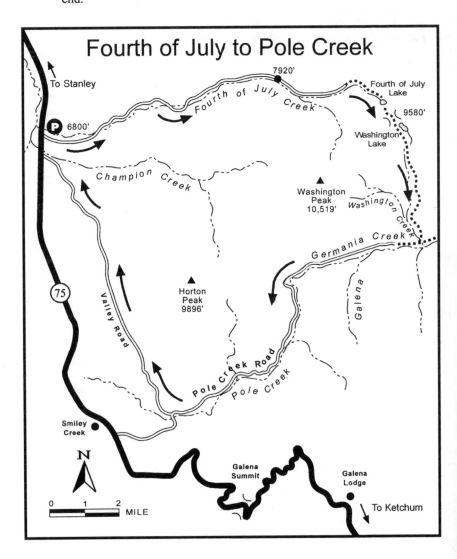

63. Fisher Creek

Length: 17.8 miles
Starting Elevation: 6625'
High Point Elevation: 8125'
Total Elevation Gain: 1500'
The Ride: Loop
Surface: Pavement, dirt jeep road and single track trail
Difficulty Rating: Difficult
Season: June - October
Fun Factor: The ultimate ride!!
Summary: When you have the time and the want for a ride that you'll be talking about for years to come, this is it. Great climbing, stream crossings and a descent that would make anyone jealous, it's all right here just waiting for you.
Getting There: From Ketchum, drive north on Highway 75 up and over Galena Summit, passing by Smiley Creek Store and Sessions Lodge to the Williams Creek Trailhead at just over 50 miles from Ketchum. If coming from Stanley, drive south on Highway 75 for approximately 13.5 miles to the turn off. The parking area is on the east side of the highway. Park here and gear up.

<u>Miles</u>	<u>The Ride:</u>
0.0	Begin by riding up the highway (south) back toward the direction you just came from.
2.3	Turn left onto Fisher Creek Road and begin a gradual cruise up the road for 6.5 miles.
8.4	Begin a very 'rideable' climb which tops out after 1/3 mile. Don't worry if you have to push your bike for a few feet. This is the only place in the ride if you have to.
9.1	You're at the top. Please register yourself so the USFS can keep tabs on the number of riders/hikers per year, and get ready for the ultimate in downhill pleasure. Be sure to take the single-track trail leading west off this saddle.
10.6	Fork in the trail. Take the left fork and continue on the Fisher Creek Loop which gradually winds and climbs its way up the small valley. The right fork leads to Warm Springs Meadow.
12.7	Another saddle. From here be careful and enjoy the bobsled descent for the next 3+ miles.
16.0	Cross over the bridge/creek and into a pristine meadow for a little regrouping. Continue left and up toward a small switchback (all rideable) and begin a fairly small climb.
16.4	Top of the last climb and only descending lies ahead. Be sure to take in the view of the Sawtooths in the last clearing before the end of the ride. You'll know where I mean.
17.8	End of the ride at Williams Creek Trailhead.

(This trail sponsored by Team Smiley Creek)

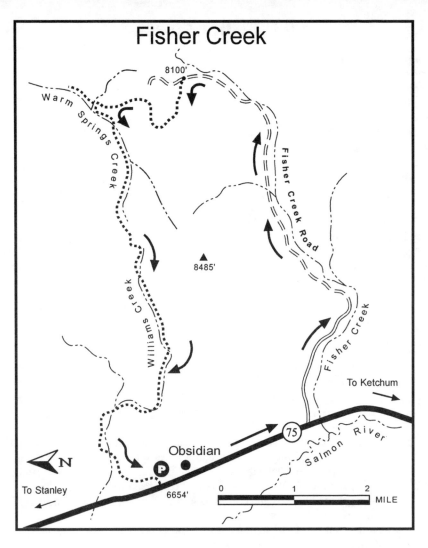

Fisher Creek

8100'

Warm Springs Creek

Williams Creek

Fisher Creek Road

▲ 8485'

Fisher Creek

To Ketchum

75

Salmon River

Obsidian

P

N

To Stanley

6654'

| 0 | | 1 | | 2 |
MILE

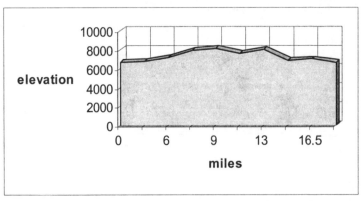

elevation

10000
8000
6000
4000
2000
0

0   6   9   13   16.5

miles

64. Redfish Lake to Decker Flats

Length: 16.8 miles
Starting Elevation: 6570'
High Point Elevation: 7680'
Total Elevation Gain: 1110'
The Ride: Loop
Surface: Single track trail, dirt jeep road and pavement
Difficulty Rating: Difficult
Season: May - October
Fun Factor: Beautiful views of Sawtooth Mountains and wildlife.
Summary: This is the ride for viewing morning and afternoon wildlife and mountains. Starting with a roller-coaster ride of technical single-track to a roving jeep trail back to the Redfish Lake road.
Getting There: From Ketchum drive North on Hwy 75 to the Redfish Lake Road turn-off (approx. 55 miles). From Stanley, drive south on Highway 75 for just over 4 miles. At 2 miles down the road pass the Redfish Lodge sign and continue to the Sandy Beach boat ramp parking lot and park here.

Miles	The Ride:
0.0	Continue on down the paved road toward Sockeye Campground passing Mt. Heyburn Campground on the way.
0.25	Turn left on the one-way road (the wrong way...clockwise).
0.33	Turn left onto the single track trail #045 with the sign pointing to "Decker Flats," and pass behind the campground restrooms.
0.8	Begin a gradual roller-coaster, climbing steep sections at times but always rideable.
1.0	Encounter the first set of switchbacks.
1.5	More switchbacks leading to more fun roller-coaster climbing.
1.8	Gain the summit ridge and check out the beautiful views of the Sawtooths, Stanley basin and Redfish Lake. Please watch for horses along this section.
2.05	Sign for Elk Meadow turns left, stay straight on the main trail.
2.7	Turn left onto the Decker Flats trail #400 and continue down the single track trail, which is an outrageous downhill.
5.4	After a fun descent down the ridge line through lodgepole pines and boulders, encounter an open meadow with great views of Decker Flats.
5.8	At the gate (please close it behind you) continue down the trail.
6.0	Junction with Decker Flats Road, turn left on the jeep road. On the right a few feet away is Huckleberry Creek and a great picnic or soaking spot.
13.2	After 7.2 miles of roller-coaster jeep trail, you come to a 5-way road junction, but keep going straight as the road winds around heading toward Redfish Lake Road.
13.8	Junction with Redfish Lake Road. Turn left and follow your original route in to the Sandy Beach boat ramp with plenty of places to take a dip in either the lakes or the creek on your cruise back.
16.8	The end of the ride and back at the Sandy Beach boat ramp.

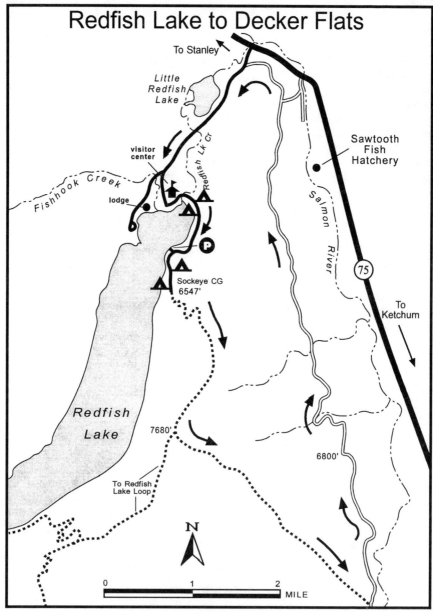

Redfish Lake to Decker Flats

To Stanley

Little Redfish Lake

visitor center

Fishhook Creek

Redfish Lk Cr

lodge

Sockeye CG
6547'

Redfish Lake

7680'

To Redfish Lake Loop

Sawtooth Fish Hatchery

Salmon River

75

To Ketchum

6800'

N

0   1   2
MILE

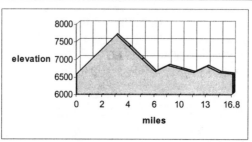

elevation

8000
7500
7000
6500
6000

0   2   4   6   8   10   13   16.8

miles

65. Redfish Lake Loop

Length: 13.9 miles
Starting Elevation: 6550'
High Point Elevation: 7560'
Total Elevation Gain: 1940'
The Ride: Loop
Surface: Single track trail and pavement
Difficulty Rating: Difficult
Season: Mid June - October
Fun Factor: Beautiful views of White Cloud Mountains, wildlife and the lake!
Summary: The loop around Redfish may seem like a little afternoon jaunt, but don't let the map fool you. This is a difficult, technical ride that'll make you beg the campers at the far end of the lake for food.
Getting There: From Ketchum drive North on Hwy 75 to the Redfish Lake Road turn-off (approx. 55 miles). From Stanley, drive south on Highway 75 for just over 4 miles. At 2 miles down the road pass the Redfish Lodge sign and junction on the right. Just past this junction on the main road is a parking area on the right. Park/start here.

Miles	The Ride:
0.0	Begin by riding out of the parking area heading south on the paved road toward Sockeye Campground.
1.6	After passing by Sandy Beach and Mt. Heyburn Campground, turn into Sock eye Campground and go left (the wrong way) onto the one-way road. Turn left onto the single track trail #045 with the sign pointing to "Decker Flats", and pass behind the campground bathrooms.
2.1	Begin a gradual roller-coaster, climbing steep sections at times but always rideable.
3.1	Gain the summit ridge and check out the beautiful views of the Sawtooths, Stanley basin and Redfish Lake. Please watch for horses along this section.
3.3	Sign for Elk Meadow turns left, stay straight on the main trail.
4.0	Sign for Decker Flats trail #400 on left. Stay on the main trail along the ridge.
5.9	At the signed junction, turn right and down towards the lake.
7.8	A very techy section, be careful of the wet rocks and logs close to the lake.
8.0	Junction: stay right on the main trail or take hike on the left trail to some falls.
8.2	In a tree'd and washy area look for the bridge crossing the creek and follow that trail around and behind the Inlet Campground. Follow this trail along the fence next to the campground, then you will start to ride away from the camp ground along the lake.
9.4	Junction: At the switchback, stay right and continue climbing up.
10.6	Just past the top of the climbing is a trail junction. The left trail leads to Bench Lakes. Stay along the ridge on the main trail heading down.
13.5	Junction: Stay right and down along Fishhook Creek. Shortly afterward, a small trail leads to the left to the Redfish Corrals, don't go there either.
13.8	Cross over the paved road and continue to the parking area.
13.9	The parking area, your car and the end of another epic, fun ride!

Redfish Lake Loop

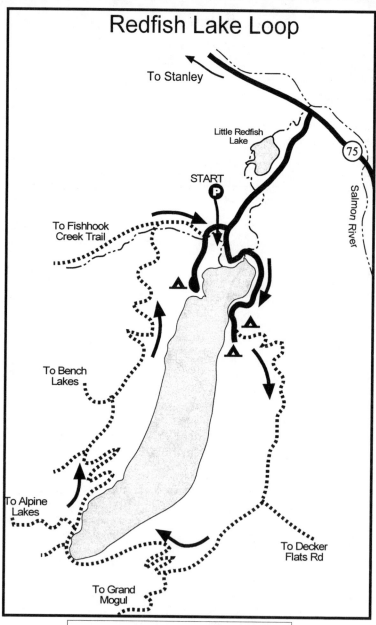

To Stanley

Little Redfish Lake

75

Salmon River

START
P

To Fishhook Creek Trail

To Bench Lakes

To Alpine Lakes

To Decker Flats Rd

To Grand Mogul

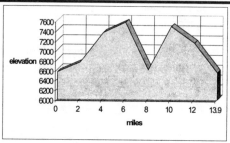

elevation

miles

66. Stanley Lake

Length: 14.2 miles
Starting Elevation: 6350'
High Point Elevation: 7400'
Total Elevation Gain: 1050'
The Ride: Out and back
Surface: Gravel road, single track trail
Difficulty Rating: Easy/Moderate
Season: June - September
Fun Factor: Gorgeous views of the Sawtooth Mountains.
Summary: This ride can give you the views, waterfalls, the Sawtooth Mountains and a lake to swim in.
Getting There: From Stanley, drive west on Highway 21 for five miles and park on the left side of the road at the beginning of the Stanley Lake Road. This is where the ride begins. You can also just drive up the road to the lake and forget potential traffic.

Miles	**The Ride:**
0.0	Begin by riding along the main road heading west toward Stanely Lake. climb slowly through the forest and be sure to stay on the main road to the lake.
3.5	Go left on the road heading toward the boat launch and pass by the Inlet Campground. Ride toward the Alpine Way Trailhead. If you accidentally turned right instead, you're on the Elk Mtn Loop ride. See ride #60 for details.
3.6	This is where you need to use your conscious environmental head. If the trail ahead of you is too muddy or simply flowing over with water, don't continue on. The erosion you could cause will last many years. However, if the trail is looking good, sign in at the registration box, go through the fence, and proceed through some rideable sand for a short stretch. Over the next couple of miles, you will encounter several water boggs and marshy areas. Be sure to carry your bike over these areas.
4.8	The Alpine Way Trail goes off to the left and enters the Sawtooth Wilderness Area. The SWA is off-limits to mountain bikes, but a great place for a hike on another day. Stay straight on the main trail.
5.3	You will encounter Stanley Lake Creek crossing, or river crossing if it's early in the summer. The trail becomes a bit more technical here, climbing through some rocky areas.
7.1	Trail junction and the top of the ride. Take the trail to the right to go check out Bridalveil Falls. The left fork enters the Sawtooth Wilderness Area again. Turn around here and enjoy the ride back down to your car.
14.2	The end of the ride.

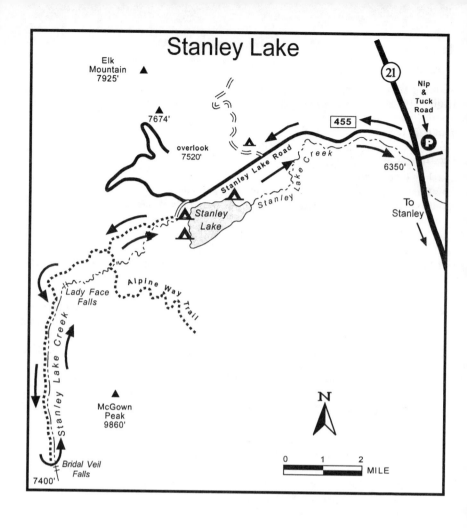

Stanley Lake

Elk
Mountain
7925'

7674'

overlook
7520'

455

Nip
&
Tuck
Road

21

P

Stanley Lake Road

Stanley Lake Creek

6350'

To
Stanley

Stanley
Lake

Alpine Way Trail

Lady Face
Falls

Stanley Lake Creek

McGown
Peak
9860'

N

Bridal Veil
Falls
7400'

0   1   2
MILE

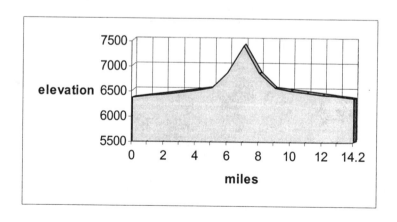

elevation

7500
7000
6500
6000
5500

0   2   4   6   8   10   12   14.2
miles

67. Elk Mountain

Length: 12.4 miles
Starting Elevation: 6550'
High Point Elevation: 7000'
Total Elevation Gain: 450'
The Ride: Loop
Surface: Dirt jeep road and single track trail
Difficulty Rating: Moderate
Season: June - October
Fun Factor: Wildlife, wildflowers, rocks, roots and mountains.
Summary: With gorgeous views and plenty of wildlife, you get Elk Mountain loop. Bring bug juice, food and a camera.
Getting There: From Stanley, drive west on Highway 21 for five miles and turn left on Stanley Lake Road #455. Drive just over 3.5 miles (passing by the Inlet C.G.) to the Elk Mountain Road #649 and park in the day-use area. The ride begins here.

Miles	The Ride:
0.0	Begin by riding up Elk Mountain road, which is a gradual grind up.
1.8	Whoa! Look left for the Elk Meadow Loop trailhead and turn left here. If you want a real grind, continue up the main road to the top for a great view after another 1.3 miles and 600 feet. The trail from here becomes rather technical going over rocks and tree roots all the while descending.
3.5	Whoa! Welcome to Elk Meadows. Be careful not to continue into the meadow and get inundated with skeeters, elk and mud. Instead, take the faint trail to the right while staying on the right or east side of the meadow.
5.2	Turn right on the trail paralleling Elk Creek, which ascends gradually through the trees, becoming a jeep trail after awhile.
6.5	You reach a dip in the road and a junction. Continue forward and down contouring the mountain. Hold on, this is some fun, fast downhill cruising! If you were to turn left here, you would reach Elk Creek and a snowmobile bridge shortly. That is the wrong way.
9.8	Trail junction: go left and shortly thereafter, up the small hill.
11.2	After cruising through a camping area, join Stanley Lake Road. Go right and follow the road back to your car at the day-use area.
12.4	The end of the ride and back at your car.

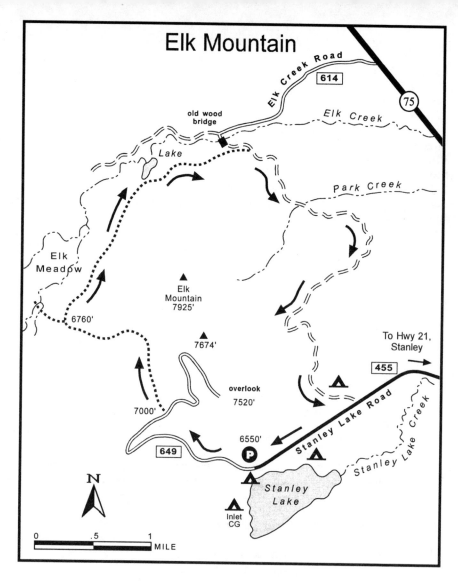

Elk Mountain

Elk Creek Road
614
75

Elk Creek

old wood
bridge

Lake

Park Creek

Elk
Meadow

Elk
Mountain
7925'

6760'

7674'

overlook
7520'

To Hwy 21,
Stanley

455

7000'

649

6550'

Stanley Lake Road

Stanley Lake Creek

N

Stanley
Lake

Inlet
CG

0   .5   1
MILE

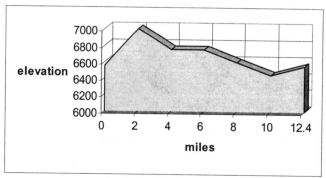

elevation

miles

168

68. Valley Creek-Knapp Creek Loop

Length: 21.1 miles
Starting Elevation: 6647'
High Point Elevation: 7290'
Total Elevation Gain: 643'
The Ride: Loop
Surface: Dirt jeep road and single-track trail
Difficulty Rating: Easy/Moderate
Season: June - October
Fun Factor: Elk, beautiful meadows, killer trail and the mountains.
Summary: This is a ride you will remember at least 'til the next one. Actually, this is a modified ATV trail that kicks some serious mountain biking butt! It is mellow and fun!
Getting There: From Stanley, drive west on Highway 21 for 11.1 miles and turn right on Rd #203. At 11.9 miles you'll pass the Blind Summit sign, and at 14.3 miles, turn right and park close to the sign pointing to Valley Creek trailhead. The ride starts here.

<u>Miles</u>	<u>The Ride:</u>
0.0	Begin by continuing up the road toward the Valley Creek trailhead.
0.9	At the obvious junction, stay to the left.
1.6	Another junction, stay to the right here.
2.4	Yet another junction, stay right here too.
3.1	Ah, finally, the Valley Creek trailhead. Seriously, it gets incredible from here!
7.3	Here you encounter a small climb.
7.8	Prospect Creek is on the right. Stay straight.
8.6	Major Junction: Go right toward Cape Horn Guard Station and Knapp Creek.
9.2	Big creek crossing over Knapp Creek, followed by another major junction. Take a left here toward the Cape Horn Guard Station.
11.4	Stay left at the junction and continue following Knapp Creek down. The trail leading off to the right goes to Winnemucca Creek.
14.5	The Knapp Creek trailhead. Follow the gravel-dirt road down to Cape Horn.
18.6	At USFS #203 (the first main road), stay left and start looking for elk grazing in the evenings and mornings.
19.3	Pass by the Cape Horn Guard Station on the left.
21.1	Hey look! Is that your car? If so, the ride is over. If not, you're lost and refer to the map for more information. Now pay attention next time, huh?

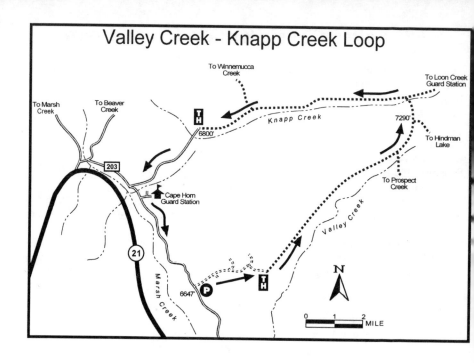

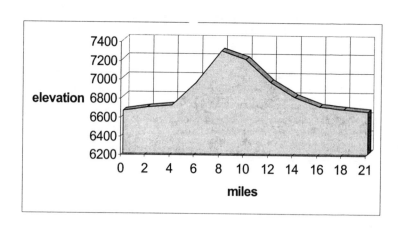

69. Winnemucca Creek-Beaver Creek Loop

Length: 13.4 miles
Starting Elevation: 6850'
High Point Elevation: 7900'
Total Elevation Gain: 1050'
The Ride: Loop
Surface: Dirt jeep road and single-track trail
Difficulty Rating: Moderate
Season: June - October
Fun Factor: Elk, beautiful meadows, killer trail and the mountains.
Summary: This is a another ride you will remember at least 'til the next one. This is another modified ATV trail that is seriously fun! Aside from the few climbs it is fairly mellow and extremely gorgeous.
Getting There: From Stanley, drive west on Highway 21 for 18 miles and turn right into the Seafoam Area. As the road forks, stay right again immediately. At 18.5 miles, bear left toward Beaver Creek Campground. Then at 23.8 miles turn right toward Loon Creek Guard Station. And at 26.7 miles from Stanley and 8.3 miles from Highway 21, park on the right in the primitive camping area on the right just before crossing over Beaver Creek. The ride begins here.

Miles	The Ride:
0.0	Begin by continuing up the main road you just came in on and over Beaver Creek. After a little climb and 0.1 miles, turn right toward Winnemucca Creek.
0.8	Trail junction: The right fork leads over to Knapp Creek, but instead continue on the main trail heading up Winnemucca Creek.
5.5	The trail begins to gradually climb a bit from here.
6.0	A short, steep climb enters the picture followed by more gradual climbing.
6.5	Ah, the top of the climbing portion of the ride. It's all downhill from here!
7.2	At the short marshy area, please be cautious of eroding the trail anymore than it already is. After this, you encounter a short, steep hill followed immediately by a crossing of Beaver Creek.
7.8	Trail junction: Stay left here and continue down the trail descending Beaver Creek.
9.5	Trail junction with Beaver Creek Trail, stay left and continue down.
9.8	The single-track trail ends at Beaver Creek Road. Stay left here and cruise down the road toward your car.
13.4	The end of the ride and back at your car. Hope you had as much fun as we did.

Winnemucca Creek-Beaver Creek Loop

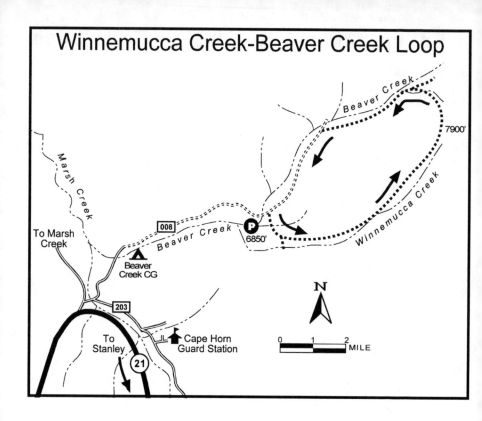

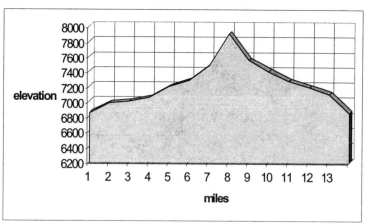

70. Wyoming Creek

Length: 25.6 miles
Starting Elevation: 6980'
High Point Elevation: 8400'
Total Elevation Gain: 2360'
The Ride: Loop
Surface: Dirt jeep road and single-track trail
Difficulty Rating: Difficult
Season: Mid-June - October
Fun Factor: You will be in an area that most people only dream of seeing.
Summary: You go from pavement to jeep road and then to single track working you from the start to the finish. You will be tired, thirsty and hungry for more. This is an amazing adventure ride!
Getting There: From Stanley, drive west on Highway 21 for 24.2 miles and park on the right in the pull-out just past the turn to Bull Trout Lake. The ride begins here.

Miles	The Ride:
0.0	Begin by riding back down Hwy 21 for 2.8 miles and turn left onto Boundary Creek Road and ride to the summit.
5.9	The top of Boundary Creek Road. Go down and stay on the main road.
8.3	Fir Creek Trail takes off to the left, stay on the road. This trail actually intersects Wyoming Creek Trail near it's summit.
11.4	Enter into Bruce Meadows and go by the landing strip shortly.
12.5	Rest area. Stay on the main road heading south toward Wyoming Creek.
13.6	Turn left on Wyoming Creek Road, just after a left side spur road.
14.4	The official Wyoming Creek Trailhead. Follow the single track trail.
18.8	Junction with Fir Creek Trail on the left. Continue up Wyoming Creek Trail.
19.0	The top of the climbing and 8400'.
20.5	Enter into the burned-out matchstick forest. Watch for sandy soil.
22.0	The trail goes up and over the ridge in a sort of hike-a-bike...it's quick!
22.6	The top of the ridge. It's all downhill from here!
24.7	Trail junction with the main trail leading toward Bull Trout Lake area. Stay on the main trail and into the parking area. Then follow that road back out to Highway 21.
27.7	Junction with Highway 21, turn right and your car should be right there on the shoulder. This is the end of the ride.

Wyoming Creek

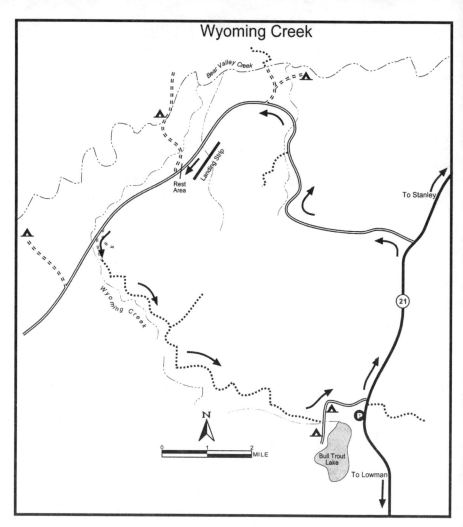

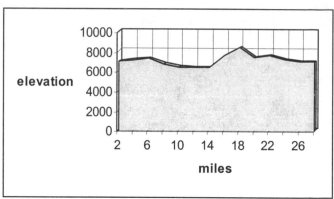

71. Nip & Tuck to Joe's Gulch

Length: 16.8 miles
Starting Elevation: 6350'
High Point Elevation: 7000'
Total Elevation Gain: 650'
The Ride: Loop
Surface: Dirt jeep road and pavement
Difficulty Rating: Moderate
Season: May - October
Fun Factor: Great views, wildlife and a fun, cruiser of a ride.
Summary: This is a casual ride with some fast downhill service followed by a bit of a grinder, but always rideable. Great views of the Sawtooth Mountains are everywhere.
Getting There: From Stanley, drive west on Highway 21 for five miles to Stanley Creek Road, turn right and park here next to Valley Creek.

<u>Miles</u>	<u>The Ride:</u>
0.0	Begin by riding up Stanley Creek Road heading north and winding around the base of the hills. Stay on this main road for the next 1.5 miles.
1.5	Trail junction: There should be a big USFS bulletin board, this tells you that, yes, you are where you should be. If it's not there, no worries, stay straight (not left) and continue on the main road. This bulletin board is the ending point of your loop before heading back to your car. Remember, always stay on the main road.
3.9	Gain a small summit and take in the views of the peaks.
6.7	After a fast descent, welcome to Lower Stanley (town) and Highway 75. Turn left here on Highway 75.
7.7	Turn left up and into Joe's Gulch. Climbing steadily but always rideable passing an old mine to a switchback.
10.1	Gain the saddle, take a quick breath and take the main road which is not left or right, but center. The other roads lead nowhere.
11.6	After reaching the high point and descending, turn left with the main road onto Kelly Creek Road #431.
12.3	Trail junction: Be sure to stay left here following the gravity of Stanley Creek.
15.0	Trail junction: Turn left here and go another 0.3 miles to the USFS brown bulletin board.
15.3	The bulletin board (maybe). Turn right here and follow your original tracks back to your car at the head of Stanley Creek Road and Highway 21.
16.8	End of the ride.

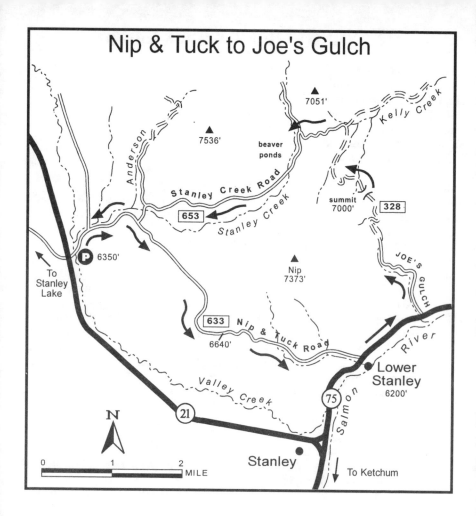

Nip & Tuck to Joe's Gulch

7051'

7536'

beaver ponds

Kelly Creek

Stanley Creek Road

653

Stanley Creek

summit 7000'

328

Anderson

JOE'S GULCH

Nip 7373'

P 6350'

To Stanley Lake

633 Nip & Tuck Road

6640'

Valley Creek

Salmon River

Lower Stanley 6200'

N

75

21

Stanley

To Ketchum

0   1   2
MILE

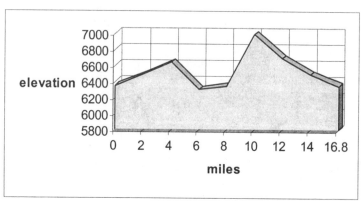

elevation

7000
6800
6600
6400
6200
6000
5800

0 2 4 6 8 10 12 14 16.8

miles

72. Little Basin Creek Loop

Length: 14.3 miles
Starting Elevation: 6600'
High Point Elevation: 7450'
Total Elevation Gain: 1250'
The Ride: Loop
Surface: Dirt jeep road and single-track
Difficulty Rating: Moderate
Season: June - October
Fun Factor: The feeling of being in the middle of nowhere, but you're not...really.
Summary: This is destined to be another Fisher Creek ride someday. Get there before the crowds do. Amazing downhills, fun climbs and if you bonk the wolves will take care of you. Just kidding.
Getting There: From Stanley, drive west on Highway 21 for five miles to Stanley Creek Road, turn right and go 1.4 miles to a big brown map board and go left. At the next junction, just over the creek, go right and follow this road for 2.9 miles (total mileage from Highway 21 is 4.3 miles. Park on the right in the clearing, the ride begins here.

Miles	The Ride:
0.0	Begin by riding up road #653. At the mining ruins at 0.4 miles, stay to the right and against the hillside on the double-track jeep trail.
1.0	Cross over Stanley Creek and the fun really begins.
2.0	The climbing begins and eases off a short distance later.
2.5	Top of the climbing and the downhill begins into Little Basin Creek...yehaa!
2.8	Enter into a gigantic meadow. Careful of the elk!
3.6	Junction with Little Basin Creek. Follow the single-track downhill from here.
5.6	After the luge-style downhill, be careful of the boulder field.
7.0	Major Junction: After crossing over Basin Creek, go right at the junction and descend the Basin Creek trail. If you were to go left, you would be on the "Hay Creek - Knapp Creek Trail".
7.4	Big crossing of Basin Creek. We looked, there is NO alternative to getting wet.
8.1	Take the switchbacks up and around the muddy bog. It's a quick climb.
9.1	Pass by a trail leading up and left into Hay Creek. Stay on the main trail.
10.6	In the large meadow, look for the sign pointing to Kelly Creek. Cross Basin Creek here and begin a casual ride up Kelly Creek.
12.3	At the junction with the jeep road, go right and continue the casual climbing.
14.3	After a quick little descent, you're back at your car and the ride is over.

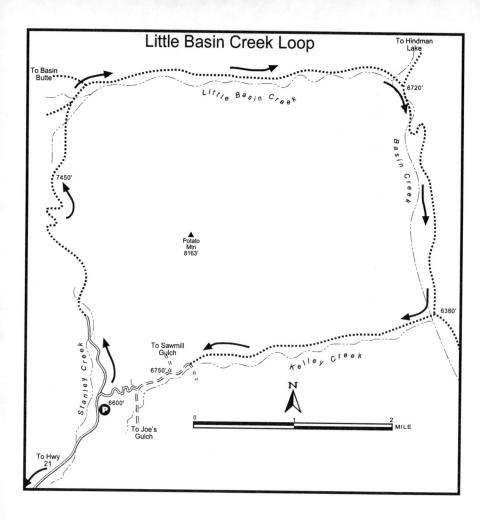

Little Basin Creek Loop

To Basin Butte

To Hindman Lake

Little Basin Creek

6720'

7450'

Basin Creek

▲ Potato Mtn 8163'

6380'

To Sawmill Gulch

Stanley Creek

6750'

Kelley Creek

P 6600'

To Joe's Gulch

N

0   1   2   MILE

To Hwy 21

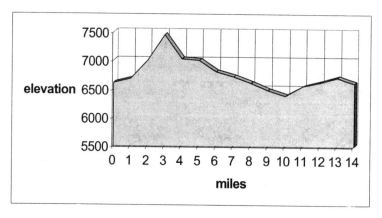

73. Basin Creek

Length: 11.4 miles
Starting Elevation: 6050'
High Point Elevation: 6650'
Total Elevation Gain: 600'
The Ride: Out and back
Surface: Dirt jeep road and single track trails
Difficulty Rating: Easy
Season: June - October
Fun Factor: Cruiser, whitewater, wild flowers, and wildlife.
Summary: Yet another sleepy little ride tucked away in the mountains around Stanley. This ride is a blast, roller-coasting your way up the valley on a jeep road and then to a single track trail.
Getting There: From Stanley, drive north on Highway 75 for 8.2 miles to the Basin Creek Campground and park on the left. The ride begins here.

Miles	The Ride:
0.0	Begin by riding up and next to the campground on the main dirt road on the north side of Basin Creek. There is a hot spring in the creek here for some good soaking after the ride.
0.7	Spur road on the right, stay on the main road at all times.
1.1	A corral on the right is the beginning of a short climb.
2.2	After crossing over a foot bridge, the road forks. Take the left fork following Basin Creek drainage.
2.7	End of the dirt road in a big turn around area. Follow the single track trail up the valley from here, roller-coastering as you go.
3.8	After crossing over a small foot bridge, there is a spur road on the right and Noho Creek on the left. Stay on the main trail heading up Basin Creek.
4.2	Kelly Creek is on the left. There is a very faint trail ascending up the Kelly Creek drainage called Noho Trail, but stay on the main trail heading up Basin Creek.
4.6	Enter into a huge meadow with a shale bridge. Pass through the meadow and please stay on the trail to prevent any unnecessary impact.
5.7	Hay Creek trail exits off to the right, which fades out shortly. This is the top of this ride, however, if you want to be a bit adventurous, continue on up the valley as far as you can go. Otherwise, turn around, head down and have some fun!
11.4	End of the ride and back at the campground.

Basin Creek

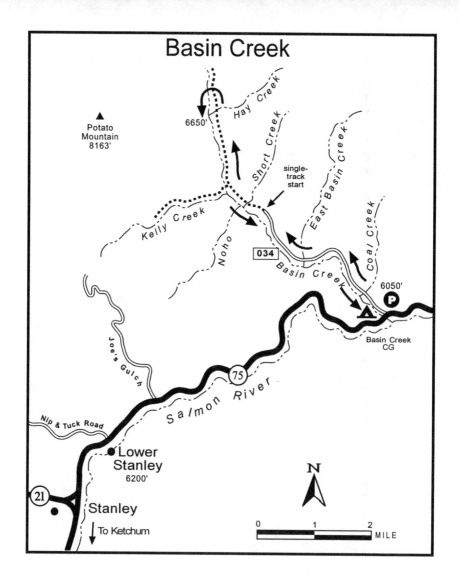

Potato Mountain 8163'

Hay Creek

Short Creek

6650'

single-track start

East Basin Creek

Coal Creek

Kelly Creek

Noho

034

Basin Creek

6050'

P

△

Basin Creek CG

Joe's Gulch

75

Salmon River

Nip & Tuck Road

Lower Stanley 6200'

21

Stanley

To Ketchum

N

0   1   2   MILE

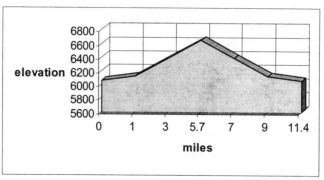

elevation

6800							
6600							
6400							
6200							
6000							
5800							
5600							

0   1   3   5.7   7   9   11.4

miles

74. Custer City

Length: 22.2 miles
Starting Elevation: 6400'
High Point Elevation: 7200'
Total Elevation Gain: 800'
The Ride: Out and back
Surface: Dirt jeep road
Difficulty Rating: Easy/Moderate
Season: May - October
Fun Factor: Old mining ruins, whitewater and wildlife.
Summary: A bit of history lies in the heart of Idaho and in the drainage of Yankee Fork Creek where you'll see an old dredge, the old Custer mining town, and ruins all along the way. It is definitely worth the ride just to learn a bit of Idaho history.
Getting There: From Ketchum, drive north on Hwy 75 to Stanley. From Stanley, drive 13 miles north on Highway 75 to Sunbeam Dam and Yankee Fork Road. Turn left here and go another 8 miles to the ghost town of Bonanza. Park anywhere near here and begin the ride.

<u>Miles</u>	<u>The Ride:</u>
0.0	Begin by riding up the main Yankee Fork Road. Head toward the famous dredge which makes a statement with the mounds of river rock all around you. You can decide for yourself what kind of statement it makes...
0.4	Just past the dredge is a spur road taking off to the left. This road leads over Loon Creek Summit and into the Frank Church River of No Return Wilderness Area. It is more suited for a long drive in the truck (4X4). Instead, stay straight on the main road heading up Yankee Fork Creek.
1.8	Ride through the old mining town of Custer City. Be sure to take some time and check out the walking tour around the town and soak up a bit of history. From here the road tends to wind through the forest next to the creek never climbing too much.
3.1	Ride over a bridge and Yankee Fork.
3.4	A Spur road on the right leads up road #73 which is the 4th of July Creek. Stay on the main road.
3.7	Pass by Custer #1 Forest Camp on the left. Begin climbing a steep pitch for 0.3 miles before the road mellows as it crosses over 5-mile creek and continues on up the valley. For the next 7 miles the ride is a nice meandering road with great valley views always following the creek.
11.1	This is the top of this ride at the Eleven Mile Barn ruins. From here it is 23 miles further if you want to continue climbing to Challis, otherwise turn around and head back down valley.
22.2	The end of the ride.

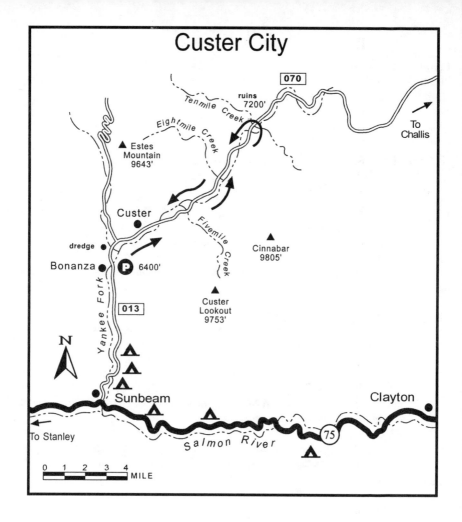

Custer City

070

ruins
7200'

Tenmile Creek

Eightmile Creek

To
Challis

▲ Estes
Mountain
9643'

Custer ●

dredge ●

Bonanza ● ●

P 6400'

Fivemile Creek

▲ Cinnabar
9805'

▲ Custer
Lookout
9753'

N

Yankee Fork

013

Sunbeam

Clayton ●

To Stanley

Salmon River

75

0 1 2 3 4
MILE

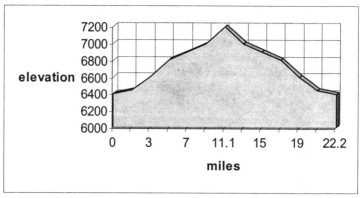

7200
7000
6800
6600
elevation 6400
6200
6000

0   3   7   11.1   15   19   22.2

miles

Multi-Day & Adventurous Rides

1. Norton Creek to Big Smoky - Starting in the Baker Creek drainage north of Ketchum, ride up and over Norton Creek into the Big Smoky drainage, eventually coming out at the Skillern Hot Springs and Big Smoky Campground, close to Featherville in the South Fork of the Boise River drainage.

2. North Fork Big Lost River to Bowery Hot Springs - Near the end of the North Fork of the Big Lost River Road, head north to Hunter Creek Summit. From here you'll descend into East Pass Creek and then to Bowery Creek. From the East Fork of the Salmon River Road, turn left and ride up to the hot springs.

3. Alturas Lake to Atlanta - From Alturas Lake on the southern end of the Sawtooth Mountains, ride up and over into the Ross Fork Basin toward Ross Fork Lakes. Turn NW into Decker Creek drainage and follow this into Atlanta. (There are other variations to this adventure, check with the USFS for trail improvements, etc.)

4. Little Casino to Big Casino Loop - This trail will be getting some improvements in the coming years, so put it on your to-do list for the near future.

5. Boundary to Williams Creek - From Highway 75 near the Sawtooth Fish Hatchery, follow Boundary Creek up and over the ridgeline heading east and eventually coming out near The Meadows in Warm Springs Creek. You can either ride out north to the Salmon River or south to finish up on Fisher Creek.

6. Lick Creek - Just over Dollarhide Summit out Warm Springs Creek you'll find a one-way trail called Lick Creek. The USFS will be doing improvements on this trail in the near future.

7. Middle Fork to South Fork of Warm Springs - This has been a heinous linkage in the past, but now the USFS is creating huge trail improvements (summer 2001). The resulting ride will be a loop topping out on the ridge looking down into the Willow Creek drainage before looping around to Poison Flats and back to the start.

8. Johnstone Creek to Pioneer Cabin Loop - This is not very popular due to the trail not being very well suited for mountain bikes. Keep this in mind when you're pushing and walking your bike. Start out Hyndman Creek up East Fork Canyon and ride up Johnstone Creek to Pioneer Cabin. From there ride/walk down the east side of the cabin into the North Fork of Hyndman Creek and back to your car. Save this for when you've done everything else.

9. Hailey to Copper Basin Loop - From Hailey, ride out Quigley Canyon, up and over into the Little Wood River drainage. Turn up Porcupine Creek and into the headwaters of the Little Wood River. Drop down to the Copper Creek Trail and into Copper Basin. How you get back is up to you.

10. Hindman Lake - From Basin Creek Campground on the Salmon River, ride up the creek to Hindman Lake. From there you can either ride back down the same way, or take the trail to Basin Butte, eventually coming down by Nip & Tuck outside Stanley. This would be a very long one-day ride. Always have a back-up plan.

11. Couch Summit to Big Smoky - From the top of Couch Summit by the Soldier Mountains, follow the jeep road across the ridges before dropping down into Miller Creek just outside of the Big Smoky Campground.

12. The Warm Springs Trail - From Bull Trout Lake outside Stanley on Highway 20, follow Dead Man Creek (Warm Springs Trail) all the way down to Bonneville Hot Springs. Don't be fooled into thinking this is an easy downhill ride, or you'll really get worked!